CHESAPEAKE
LEGENDS
AND LORE
FROM THE
WAR OF 1812

CHESAPEAKE
LEGENDS
AND LORE
FROM THE
WAR OF 1812

RALPH E. ESHELMAN & SCOTT S. SHEADS

Charleston   London

THE
History
PRESS

Published by The History Press
Charleston, SC 29403
www.historypress.net

Front cover: The U.S. Chesapeake Flotilla being chased by a vastly superior British squadron off the mouth of the Patuxent River during an afternoon squall on June 1, 1814. © *Richard Schlecht*. *Back cover*: The much-hated British rear admiral George Cockburn stands before his handiwork, an embellished version of the burning of Washington in 1814. *Courtesy of National Maritime Museum, Greenwich, England.*

First published 2013

Manufactured in the United States

ISBN 978.1.62619.071.9

Library of Congress CIP data applied for.

Notice: The information in this book is true and complete to the best of our knowledge. It is offered without guarantee on the part of the authors or The History Press. The authors and The History Press disclaim all liability in connection with the use of this book.

When the legend becomes fact, print the legend.[1]

This book is published in cooperation with the Maryland War of 1812 Bicentennial Commission and the National Park Service, which administers the Star-Spangled Banner National Historic Trail.

The Star-Spangled Banner National Historic Trail commemorates the events and legacy of the War of 1812 in the Chesapeake along more than five hundred miles of land and water routes connecting parks, museums and historic sites that provide learning and recreation opportunities for residents and visitors.

Contents

CONTENTS

CONTENTS

Preface

This book grew out of research we have been conducting over the past two decades. What began as an effort to document all of the War of 1812 veterans buried in Maryland grew into a book on the historic sites related to the war in the Chesapeake.* That publication, co-authored with Donald Hickey, resulted in *The War of 1812 in the Chesapeake: A Reference Guide To Historic Sites In Maryland, Virginia, and the District of Columbia*. In writing that book, it was often difficult to separate fact from legend. There were scores of fascinating stories, but for many, no primary documentation could be found to support them. How could we include such stories without proof of their authenticity? When in doubt, we included words such as "reportedly," "supposedly" or "reputedly" to let the reader know that the story might or might not be true.

Many of the more farfetched stories, such as militiamen* using a catapult made from pine saplings to attack a British barge, were not used. Did a young boy really fool the British into believing a wasp nest was a hummingbird nest? Did the British shoot a pet monkey during a raid? This book is a collection of legends, myths, tales and lore about real and fabricated events during the War of 1812. There are so many such examples that this book may be considered a first volume. If enough interest is generated, one or more additional volumes can be added—the stories are that plentiful.

For those wanting to learn more about the War of 1812 in the Chesapeake, readers are encouraged to explore the several fine books on this subject, many of which are available at your local library. Among them is *In Full Glory*

Reflected: Discovering The War of 1812 in the Chesapeake (Maryland Historical Society Press and Maryland Historical Trust Press, 2012). This book is written for the general public, is well illustrated and provides an overall history of the war in the Chesapeake. For those wanting to travel to War of 1812 sites in the Chesapeake, see *A Travel Guide to The War of 1812 in the Chesapeake: Eighteen Tours in Maryland, Virginia, and the District of Columbia* (The Johns Hopkins University Press, 2011). Another recommended resource is the Star-Spangled Banner National Historic Trail webpage at www.starspangledtrail.net. The trail commemorates the events and legacy of the War of 1812 in the Chesapeake along more than five hundred miles of land and water routes connecting parks, museums and historic sites that provide learning and recreation opportunities for residents and visitors.

With the bicentennial of the War of 1812 upon us, more than one hundred new books were published on the subject in 2012, with more to come over the next two years. Nearly all of them are scholarly accounts about some aspect of the war. This volume is meant to be an entertaining book that offers insights into the origins of these legends and lore. We hope you will enjoy it and also gain an awareness of how history is sometimes derived from fabricated stories that have become so ingrained in our traditions that they have become "fact."

Ralph E. Eshelman, Preston Point, Calvert County, Maryland
Scott S. Sheads, Locust Point, Baltimore, Maryland
February 2013

Acknowledgements

The authors gratefully recognize the following individuals for their assistance in providing information and helping to make this book possible: Paul Berry, Stuart Butler, Suzanne Copping, James Dawson, Steve Frohock, Christopher George, Kevin Hemstock, Donald Hickey, Silas Hurley, Pete Himmelheber, Ross Kimmel, Burton Kummerow, Larry Leone, Cecilia Malin, John Maounis, John Mccavitt, Bill Pencek, Robert Reyes and Ed Seufert. We are indebted to the Maryland Historical Society for use of images from their vast collections and to Robert Papp for allowing us to use one of his illustrations from *The Town That Fooled the British: A War of 1812 Story*, a children's book written by his wife, Lisa Papp. Some of the illustrations in this book were produced by Gerry Embleton and Richard Schlecht and are used here in cooperation with the Maryland War of 1812 Bicentennial Commission and the National Park Service, which administers the Star-Spangled Banner National Historic Trail.

Introduction

"If people want to cite the lessons of history, they need to get the history right in the first place." [2]
—*Glenn Kessler, 2012*

Legends and lore are known from around the world, some dating from oral traditions passed on over a multitude of generations. Others are more recent, dating from within our current generation. Legends and lore are often used to explain events or circumstances that may or may not have taken place. Legends and lore sometimes reinforce moral and social values. The *Webster's Collegiate Dictionary* defines a myth as a "traditional story of ostensibly historical events…a popular belief or tradition that has grown up around something or someone…an unfounded or false notion…a person or thing having only an imaginary or unverifiable existence." The same dictionary defines a legend as a "story coming down from the past; one popularly regarded as historical although not verifiable…a popular myth of recent origin." The definition of lore is "traditional knowledge or belief." [3] Lore encompasses oral histories, proverbs, popular beliefs, fairy tales, stories, tall tales and customs.

The War of 1812 has its share of legends and lore. Donald Graves, a noted Canadian War of 1812 scholar, states, "The War of 1812 is a conflict that carries an unduly heavy burden of mythology, much of it propagated by nineteenth-century historians and deriving mainly from national chauvinism." [4] In *Don't Give Up the Ship!: Myths of the War of 1812*,

American War of 1812 scholar Donald Hickey is laudatory of the wealth of information provided in Benson J. Lossing's work *The Pictorial Field-Book of the War of 1812* but is also critical of some of Lossing's methods:

> *After doing some preliminary research in the 1850s, he* [Lossing] *traveled some 10,000 miles in the United States and Canada, examining archival material, talking to veterans, and sketching people, battlefields and other sites and scenes. Lossing's study…has a wealth of information, and despite its antiquarian flavor, it remains useful today. On the other hand, he uncritically repeated a great many tales that he heard, and as a result, his work did much to fix and popularize myths touching on many aspects of the war.*[5]

The Chesapeake also has a wealth of legends and lore. For examples, see George Alfred Townsend's *Tales of the Chesapeake*, first published in 1880; Annie Weston Whitney and Caroline Canfield Bullock's "Folk-Lore from Maryland" in *Memoirs of the American Folklore Society*; George G. Carey's *Maryland Folklore and Folklife*; Charles A. Mills's *Treasure Legends of Virginia*; Helena Lefroy Caperton's *Legends of Virginia*; and Thomas E. Barden's *Virginia Folk Legends*.

The purpose of this book is to explore the legends and lore from the Chesapeake that pertain to the War of 1812. A century after the War of 1812 had ended, the Star-Spangled Banner National Centennial Committee was formed to plan and carry out celebrations to commemorate Maryland's role in that war. These centennial celebrations furthered the legends and lore of the War of 1812. In succeeding generations, these stories, whether published or passed on orally, became part of the popular culture of the region.

Legends and lore about the War of 1812 have become an accepted part of the Chesapeake's history and have been interwoven into the very fabric of documented history. These stories are retold here with one important difference: instead of merely gathering and retelling the legends and lore, we researched their origins as best we could. The available facts sometimes support the legend or tale and at other times discredit them. Some will no doubt be pleased at what we found, others will be disappointed and some will dispute our findings. Traditions are hard to break even when the facts don't support them.

Perhaps the best-known Maryland Eastern Shore tale was that in 1813, the residents of St. Michaels hung "lanterns in the trees and mastheads of ships" to fool the British as to the actual distance of the town from the enemy warship, causing the British gunners in the darkness to overshoot the

Washington Crossing the Delaware is an 1851 painting by German-American artist Emanuel Gottlieb Leutze. The original painting was destroyed during a British air raid in 1942. A second version of this painting by Leutze survives at the Metropolitan Museum of Art in New York. *Courtesy of Metropolitan Museum of Art.*

town and thus spare it harm. This tale, told repeatedly to bolster tourism, is not supported by documentary evidence. It appears to be the confused memory of an old veteran, recounted decades after the event actually occurred. Likewise, while it is widely held that the British burned the city of Washington in 1814, they actually burned fewer than 20 of the more than 350 structures in the city at that time. The American military burned the Washington Navy Yard, which consisted of as many if not more structures than the British, to keep war supplies and weapons out of enemy hands.

These stories and others have been told so often that for many they have become an accepted part of the Chesapeake's history. They are similar to the Revolutionary War stories of Betsy Ross sewing the first American flag (she didn't) or George Washington draping himself with an American flag as he stood in the bow of a boat while crossing the Delaware River during the American Revolutionary War (he didn't stand or wrap a flag around him). These stories have become legends, and while they have no factual basis, they continue to be retold two hundred years later.

The epigraph for this book is taken from the 1962 film *The Man Who Shot Liberty Valance*, the story of a young lawyer in a rough cattle town who, by a series of events, shot the local gunslinger Liberty Valance. His notoriety in the years after this daring deed propelled him to territorial, state and national politics—all based on the belief that he killed Liberty Valance. As the film later reveals, it was a local rancher known for his roughness and fast gun who saved the lawyer's life by ambushing Valance from an alley. In the darkness of the night and commotion that followed, the young lawyer received the credit. The rancher later told the lawyer what really happened; that he had shot Valance to save the lawyer's life. When questioned later by a newsman about his early life, the lawyer told the real story and that he did not deserve the rewards that had propelled him to fame, but the reporter refused to tell the true story, replying, "When the legend becomes fact, print the legend."

METHODOLOGY

In order to attempt to resolve the truth of a legend or lore, we first sought the original source. We found that few legends and lore actually date from the war itself. This is not surprising, since legends and lore are often the result of trying to explain something that took place earlier in time, while the facts around them have been forgotten or altered over multiple repeating of the stories. Thus, while we sought contemporary documentation, our efforts were usually unsuccessful. For many of these legends and lore, the earliest records were newspaper articles written decades later, in many cases a century or more after the event was said to have taken place. For example, it has been popularly believed that the British called Baltimore a "nest of pirates" due to the number of privateering vessels built there, yet our research has found no such contemporary usage of the term "pirate" in connection with Baltimore. In fact, the earliest such usage was by a historian writing a history of Baltimore City in the 1880s. These legends and lore are now taken as fact.

One must also evaluate the source. What are the chances that an individual whose home was visited by the British during the war immediately wrote down that experience? If they did, what are the chances that the letter or diary survives today? Would their account necessarily be accurate as to the actual events that occurred at that time, or would the writer have embellished and spun the event to make them appear brave or spun the account out of

Wartime propaganda illustrating two sides of the same story—one British, one American. Which do you believe? © *Gerry Embleton illustration.*

hatred for the enemy? An account might have been orally repeated over and over before someone bothered to write it down. By then, the original story had probably changed or been embellished. Just because a newspaper publishes a letter from an individual does not necessarily mean that the letter portrays the event accurately. Were newspaper accounts back then any more accurate than those of today's newspapers? Federalist newspapers gave their reports a different spin than did the Democratic-Republican newspapers. When you compare contemporary United States newspapers with Great Britain newspapers of the time, the differences in accounts are often striking.

A pertinent example involves comparing accounts of a raid on Chaptico, St. Mary's County, Maryland, on July 30, 1814. First is a British account, followed by an American account. Judge for yourself which report more likely portrays the event accurately.

> [T]*ook possession of the Town of Chaptico—where some ladies who had heard of our good behaviour at Leonards Town remained—and sang and played on the piano. We took from thence 70 Hhds.* [hogsheads*] *of tobacco, some flour, & military stores but preserved their houses* [and] *purchased from them stock and various articles of provisions. The men all*

fled, but the ladies remained to see the wonderful [Rear] *Admrl.* [George] *Cockburn and the British folks.* (Captain Robert Rowley's report to his superiors, August 1814.)

[T]*hey* [the British] *got about 80 hhds. of tobacco and no other plunder, the inhabitants having moved all their property out of their grasp. Yet here they made a most furious attack on every window, door, and pane of glass in the village, not one was left in the whole. They picked their stolen geese in the church, dashed the pipes of the church organ on the pavement, opened a family vault in the churchyard, broke open the coffins, stirred the bones about with their hands in search of hidden treasure—all this in the presence of their worthy admiral.* (*American and Commercial Daily Advertiser*, August 12, 1814.)

These two accounts contrast so strikingly that unless one were to look at both sources, one would get a rather one-sided opinion of the event. Even the difference in the number of hogsheads of tobacco taken is different; seventy versus eighty. It is safe to say that both accounts spun the truth for the benefit of their audiences. Despite the acknowledgment that newspaper accounts may not always be reliable, many of the sources for these legends and tales are newspapers.

In conclusion, we were unable to find primary documentation to support most of the legends and lore from the Chesapeake region during the War of 1812. What we attempted to do, where we could, was to show when the legend or lore was first reported in the written record and how the facts surrounding it support or diminish that claim.

ORGANIZATION

The entries in this book are organized in alphabetical order, first by state and then by county. Thus, Maryland is first, followed by Virginia and then Washington, D.C.

Words followed by an asterisk (*) are defined in the glossary at the back of the book. Readers, especially those from Virginia, will find that the vast majority of legends and tales come from Maryland. This is not a deliberate slight to Virginia, but we simply did not find as many examples from that state. The authors are Marylanders and know their state better than Virginia. We do not claim to have visited every historical society or county library in Virginia to research their vertical history files. There are certainly more Virginia stories to be found, so we encourage readers to send them to us.

Finally, the authors welcome comments, additions and corrections. We are especially eager to hear about other legends and lore we may have overlooked, as well as any documentation that might support any of the legends and lore in this book. Please contact the authors at ree47@comcast. net or scottsheads1316@comcast.net.

Maryland

Maryland Eastern Shore

DORCHESTER COUNTY

Cake on a Silver Platter and a Goose on a Teapot

A legend from Taylors Island is that Polly Travers, accompanied by her friend Mary Gadd, had her slave row them out to a Royal Naval vessel to seek the release of her husband, John Travers, who had been captured along with his boat. Legend claims that her plea was successful in gaining the release of John but not his boat. The slave who rowed Polly out to the ship was not allowed onboard. According to the legend, during the negotiations, someone served the slave a piece of cake on a silver platter. After the cake was eaten and Polly, Mary and John embarked the rowboat for their joyous voyage home, the silver platter was forgotten, and it too was taken ashore.[6] The platter is said to have been engraved with "The *Marlborough*," the name of the ship, a seventy-four-gun Royal Navy ship of the line.* More likely the platter, if inscribed, would have had "HMS Marlborough," its proper name. Because this legend includes full names and because *Marlborough* was part of Rear Admiral George Cockburn's squadron, this story may have some basis to it, but it is hard to conceive of the British serving a slave a piece of cake on a silver platter. If the platter

Is this Polly Travers's teapot? *Ralph Eshelman photograph.*

exists, perhaps the descendants of the family can produce a photograph of it to confirm this presently unproven legend.

A second legend about Polly Travers is that when the British threatened to raid the family farm on Taylors Island, Polly hid valuables, including an heirloom silver teapot, under the nest of a setting goose. Every farm family knew one did not disturb a setting goose since she could be ferocious in protecting her nest.[7]

Descendants of the Travers family allowed Ralph Eshelman to examine the teapot. The pot is not silver but appears to be plated or Britannia metal.* It is stamped on the bottom "JAMES DIXON & SONS 1832." James Dixon and Thomas Smith began metalworking in England circa 1806. When William Frederick Dixon, the eldest son of James, joined the firm in 1823, the name of the company was changed to James Dixon & Son. When James Willis Dixon, the second son of James, joined the firm in 1835, the name was changed to James Dixon & Sons.[8] It is unclear whether the 1832 on the bottom of the teapot is a date, but because this company did not become James Dixon & Sons until well after the War of 1812, this teapot cannot be the pot Polly hid under a setting goose. The family owns two other teapots, one of which is marked 1844 and the second bears no date but appears to be from the late nineteenth century. Either the story is purely a family legend or over time, the teapot claimed to have been Polly's was misidentified.

Polly was born Mary C. Dove on April 18, 1777, and married John Critchett Travers on April 5, 1797. A lifelong resident of Taylors Island, she died in 1857. Over the generations, she became known as "Aunt" or "Grandmother," depending on who was telling the tale. It is interesting that we have two tales about Polly, each involving pieces of silver. One was a platter supposedly given to Polly's slave and the other a teapot that reputedly belonged to Polly's family. A family member stated that it was family tradition that the *Marlborough* platter had been buried with the teapot under the setting goose. We have no tangible evidence to support either of these stories, but the legends of the cake served on a silver platter and a teapot hidden under a setting goose are among the scores of fascinating stories based on the War of 1812 in the Chesapeake.

There are several similar tales of hiding valuables from the enemy by burying them. At the Fassitt House (see "The Corn Stalk Ruse at Mount Ephraim"), the owners buried their silver and then somehow forgot the exact spot. At the Trotten House (see "Poison Incidents") in North Point, the owners planted cabbages on the disturbed soil to conceal the location.[9] At the Todd House (see "British Soldiers and the Todd House Graveyard"), also in North Point, a grave was supposedly dug up because silver was believed to have been buried there.

The Battle of the Ice Mound and the Becky-Phipps Cannon

In early February 1815, HM sloop of war* *Dauntless*, anchored on the Patuxent River on the western shore of the bay, launched a ship's tender* commanded by Lieutenant Matthew Phibbs and manned by a midshipman, thirteen sailors, three Royal Marines, a black man and a black woman who served as a cook. On a very cold day, they proceeded toward the small town

Battle of the Ice Mound, the last engagement of the war in Maryland. © *Gerry Embleton illustration.*

of Tobacco Stick (present-day Madison), located on the eastern shore of the bay. The tender was armed with a twelve-pound carronade,* in addition to small arms the crew carried.

On February 6, the crew from the tender had pillaged the area, taken seven sheep from the farm of Moses Geohagan and burned several vessels. As the tender began its way back across the Chesapeake, it encountered considerable drift ice, and Phibbs decided to spend the night in the lee off nearby James Island until daylight. Early on February 7, they discovered that the tender had become ice-bound and they were frozen in. News of the tender's plight reached Private Joseph Fookes Stewart, a shipyard owner and planter who lived on James Island and served in Captain Thomas Woolford's detachment of the 48th Maryland militia.* Steward decided to engage the tender with a small group of fellow local militiamen. After a two-hour musket barrage, the British crew surrendered.

Following this action, Stewart submitted a petition for prize money to Congress, and on April 29, 1816, he and his comrades were awarded

$1,800. This last engagement of the war in Maryland has come to be known as the Battle of the Ice Mound, named after the mound of ice used by Stewart's men to defend themselves during the engagement. The carronade from the tender was taken as a trophy and nicknamed Becky Phipps, for the tender's captured black cook, Becky, and the commander, Lieutenant Phibbs. The cook's name was actually Becca, and the commander's name was Phibbs. Over time, Becca Phibbs became corrupted to Becky Phipps. It seems strange that a cannon would have been named after a British lieutenant and a black cook, but perhaps there is more to this story than we know.

The carronade became a war memorial and was used in American political celebrations. On the night of Tuesday, November 12, 1912, news was received on Taylors Island that Woodrow Wilson had been elected president of the United States. The jubilation was described as follows:

> [A] *number of enthusiastic Democrats decided to press it* [the carronade] *into service. It was hastily swapped out and its touch hole cleaned, and it was loaded and touched off. Again & again it was fired off, the charges of powder increasing each time. When it was loaded for the fourth time with two pounds of powder, it was filled up with marsh turf and oyster shells, and these rammed in until the old gun was loaded clear to the muzzle. Then it was touched off. The cannon rose in the air and turned a dozen somersaults, and parts of it went shooting off in every direction. One piece weighing about 200 pounds went sailing off and has not since been seen. The remainder of the old gun was found, but it is nothing more than scrap iron. It will never be fired again.*[10]

In 1950, the Daughters of the American Revolution (DAR) and other citizens collected what remained of the exploded carronade, assembled what they could and had the gun mounted at its present site. On July 9, 1961, a DAR marker was installed, but interestingly, it has the date of the capture of the tender as 1814, not 1815. On May 23, 1999, a year after a new Taylors Island Bridge was completed, the Maryland State Highway Department, in cooperation with the Grace Foundation of Taylors Island, re-dedicated the site by remounting the cannon, constructing a pavilion over the gun and installing a Maryland Historic Roadside Marker with the correct date of capture. The Becky Phipps tale is true, but the names have become changed over time.

Did Pewter Spoons Help Capture a British Vessel?

In 1909, a newspaper reported that when the Dorchester County militia*
attacked a "small fleet" that entered the Little Choptank River, the militia
melted pewter spoons to make bullets since they were short on lead balls for
their muskets. The article credits Colonel John C. Jones (1755–1848) as the
leader of the militia band that captured one of the enemy vessels. Following
is an extract from that article:

> *The British had entered the Chesapeake and were terrorizing the people
> along the bay and some of its tributaries. One small fleet, consisting of three
> transports, two of which were loaded with supplies for troops, and the third
> with troops, entered the Little Choptank River for safety during a storm. While
> being at anchor, the weather suddenly became intensely cold…and the wind
> banked ice on the shore, the ice flows being 8 to 10 feet high. Colonel Jones,
> whose plantation was on the river not far from the marooned vessels, took the
> situation in hand promptly. He sent his colored servants in all directions and
> summoned the people from the country within several miles.*
>
> *About 40 [illegible] farmers and fishermen had gathered by nightfall
> with their old ducking and squirrel guns and ammunition, the bullets had
> been molded from pewter spoons. Colonel Jones led his men to the shore
> and when the [British] soldiers and sailors began to show themselves on
> deck of the transports the next morning, firing again from the ice banks…
> the British held out only about 36 hours, when a white flag was raised.*[11]

This story was brought to light upon the death of Colonel Jones's
granddaughter, Miss Georgiana Fisher, in 1909. After having read the Becky-
Phipps cannon entry above, this story should sound familiar because it is a
later version of the Battle of the Ice Mound that took place on February
7, 1815. Did the militia really melt pewter spoons to make bullets for the
engagement? Based on the misinformation in the article, it is doubtful, but it
does give a nice twist to the Battle of the Ice Mound story.

Here are the problems. It was not a small fleet that got stranded in the ice;
it was only a small tender.* The biggest concern is that there is no record
of a John C. Jones having played any role in this action. His 1848 obituary
states, "The deceased served his country with distinction as lieutenant in the
'Old Maryland line' in the war of the Revolution."[12] Having been born in
1755, he would have been a young man during the American Revolution.

There was a John Jones who served as lieutenant colonel in the Dorchester County 48th Regiment, who would have been sixty years old at the time of the action, but none of the records pertaining to those present at the Battle of the Ice Mound includes a John Jones.[13]

It must be inferred that over time, the story became entangled between what Jones did in the American Revolutionary War and what he did in the War of 1812. It is doubtful that a sixty-year-old officer hid behind an ice mound to lead the local militia on a terribly cold day in February. All the accounts clearly indicate that Joseph Stewart of James Island organized and led the attack. Because of these inconsistencies, it is believed that the pewter spoon tale was subsequently added to the story to embellish it, but this cannot be verified.

KENT COUNTY

Captain Parker and His Whiskey-Filled Coffin

In the aftermath of the Battle of Caulks Field, which took place during a full moon early in the morning of August 31, 1814, discussion centered on who fired the fatal shot that killed Captain Sir Peter Parker, commander of the British force. On October 18, 1902, a granite monument was erected to commemorate the battlefield. At that time, the *Baltimore Sun* reported, "The claim is made for Henry Urie that he killed Sir Peter Parker." Urie is said to have pointed out an officer wearing white pantaloons, at which point he declared, "I'm going to shoot him."[14] The story continues:

> *This heroic leader was shot in the leg by Henry Urie, a Rock Haller* [from nearby Rock Hall], *so we were told by Justice Robert Calder* [in 1902], *whose father fought at Caulk's Field. Urie was strategically located, Justice Calder said, on the over hanging limbs of a huge willow tree where Sir Peter Parker had reined up his white battle charger. Henry Urie ambushed aloft, his blunder-buss loaded to the muzzle with all the hardware, bolts, nuts, nails, etc. in his barnyard. That one shot may have saved Chestertown.*[15]

Left: Captain Sir Peter Parker, whose body was preserved in a whiskey-filled coffin. *Courtesy of National Maritime Museum.*

Below: British sketch of Caulks Field Battlefield showing American encampment in upper left, American lines in upper center and British line in lower center. The "A" near the center of sketch was added to mark what appears to be a willow tree. *Courtesy of National Archives, United Kingdom, London.*

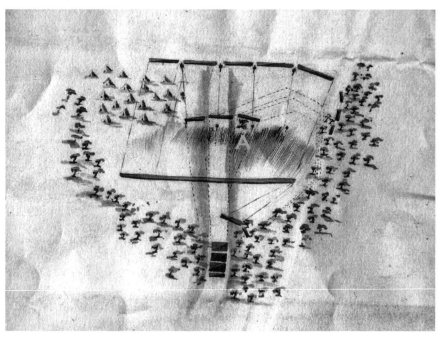

There are several problems with this story. Parker did not ride a horse at Caulks Field. This apparently is a confusion of the death of Major General Robert Ross, who did ride a horse at North Point (see "Who Killed General Ross?"). It is doubtful that a "blunder-buss" was used in the engagement. While a blunderbuss was a form of early shotgun, it was usually employed by cavalry, not riflemen. Nearby Chestertown was not on Captain Parker's (nor the British admiralty's) known list of targets during the war, and the Americans were initially unaware that Parker had even been killed. It was only when the sun rose that a blood-soaked shoe with Parker's name inside it was found on the battlefield. While Sergeant Henry Urie's name does appear on Captain Simon Wickes's Rifle Company muster roll for August 30, 1814, the same cannot be said for any citizen or soldier named Calder. No such name appears on any muster rolls of those who served in the 21st Maryland Regiment that fought that night. A search of contemporary newspapers and correspondence did not mention specifically any soldier's name who might have fired the fatal shot, only that the British commander had met his death on the battlefield. It is curious that this claim arose some eighty-eight years later.[16]

Lieutenant Henry Crease, who assumed command upon Parker's death, reported three days after the event: "It was at this time, while animating his men in the most heroic manner, that Sir Peter Parker received his mortal wound which obliged him to quit the field and he expired in a few minutes."[17] Lieutenant Colonel Philip Reed, commander of the local militia, stated in his report only one day after the engagement that "Sir Peter Parker was amongst the slain—he was mortally wounded with buck-shot and died before he reached the barges, to which he was conveyed by his men."[18] However, contemporary newspaper accounts based on a report of a wounded British soldier who was left on the field stated Captain Parker "had received a 'second' wound, which killed him."[19] If Urie could have somehow known his shot hit Captain Parker in the leg during this moonlit battle, then who fired the second shot that instantly killed him? The person who killed Captain Parker will probably never be known. It is very possible that the individual never realized his shot had delivered the mortal blow. There are no known documents that support Henry Urie having killed Captain Parker. There is a similar controversy in regards to who killed Major General Robert Ross at the Battle of North Point (see "General Ross's Last Breath").

On the *Sketch of the Battle*, drawn by Lieutenant Crease soon after the battle, there appears to be a weeping willow tree. Is this the tree Justice Calder referred to in the 1902 newspaper account? Willow trees are often symbolically used to represent mourning, and they were often engraved on tombstones in the late eighteenth and early nineteenth centuries.[20] Could Lieutenant Crease have seen a willow tree on the battlefield on that moonlit night, or was he symbolically indicating the spot of Captain Parker's death?

Captain Parker's internal organs were removed on September 1, 1814, and his body "placed into a coffin filled with whiskey." Meanwhile, Lieutenant Henry Crease sent a flag of truce onshore so that prisoners could be exchanged.[21] Six days later, on September 7, HM frigate* *Menelaus* was sighted coming down the bay from Kent County "with her pennant half-mast high, a sign indicative of the death of Sir Peter Parker," as a gathering storm and lightning augmented the solemn occasion. That evening, the remains of Captain Parker were transferred to HM frigate *Hebrus*.[22]

The British squadron, including *Hebrus*, commanded by Rear Admiral George Cockburn, arrived in Bermuda on October 8, 1814. The remains of Captain Sir Peter Parker were received with military honors and laid to rest in the burial grounds of St. George's Church. The following spring, on April 2, 1815, the body of Parker was removed and conveyed back onboard *Hebrus* via Halifax to London, where on May 14, 1815, official ceremonies laid his body in final rest at St. Margaret's Church at Westminster by the Reverend George Rennell, chaplain of HM ship of the line* *Albion*.[23]

The Mitchell House and Parker's Blanket

Near Tolchester, ten miles west of Chestertown at the end of Maryland Parkway off Maryland Route 21, is situated the Joseph Mitchell House. Built in 1743, the Mitchell House is now operated as a bed and breakfast inn. This handsome house belonged to Joseph Mitchell (d.1837), a veteran of the War of 1812 who was appointed by the state as the commissary of supplies for the Kent County Militia.*[24]

The Mitchell House has long been the center of Kent County's folklore, claiming that following the death of Captain Sir Peter Parker at the Battle of Caulks Field on August 31, 1814, British troops carried Parker's body to the Mitchell House, where they wrapped him in a blanket and sheet. Like most legends, it has been so often told that it has become regarded as fact. This story had its origins in a letter dated September 1 that was published in a Washington newspaper on September 5, 1814. The letter stated, "On their retreat, they called at a house some distance from the field of battle and got a blanket and sheet, it is supposed to wrap Sir Peter in."[25]

House from which Joseph Mitchell was taken prisoner. *Ralph Eshelman photograph.*

Apparently, the Mitchell House came to be linked to the Parker death story from a journal entry by Lieutenant Benjamin G. Benyon of HM frigate* *Menelaus*, who was with Captain Parker when he died. In the entries prior to and immediately after the battle, Lieutenant Benyon does not mention nor make any reference to stopping at any house along their return to where the British had landed from barges and where they reembarked. It was on September 3, 1814, that Benyon made his first reference to the Mitchell House:

> *At half past three o'clock,* [Lieutenant Henry] *Crease...and* [Lieutenant George] *Poe went to Major Mitchels House* [and] *found him in bed with his wife, he was soon roused out and brought off, his horses with saddles. Mitchell was the militia contractor for Kent County.*[26]

The next day, Mrs. Mitchell visited her husband onboard *Menelaus*, bringing with her "some fruit, butter, cider, etc," before the ships departed down the bay to join the British fleet off the Potomac River to begin their preparations for the attack on Baltimore.[27] On September 18, Lieutenant Colonel Philip Reed assisted Mrs. Mitchell to obtain the release of her husband by forwarding a letter informing Major General Samuel Smith that "the capturing party entered the Mitchell house and his chambers in the early morning hours of 4 September and that he was now requesting a flag-of-truce vessel for Mrs. Mitchell."[28]

Two days later, Mrs. Mitchell left Rock Hall for Baltimore with a second letter written by Lieutenant Colonel Reed seeking the release of her husband through the military offices of Major General Samuel Smith. Reed described Joseph Mitchell as "an officer of much activity and usefulness in his appointment as commissary of supplies for Kent County under the authority of the state." Despite these efforts, Joseph Mitchell was transferred to HM ship of the line* *Asia*. To the dismay of Mrs. Mitchell, her husband was apparently imprisoned in England until after the war. The Mitchell House was not visited by the British immediately after the Battle of Caulks Field. The house where the blanket and sheet came from is unknown but was probably located along Georgetown Road, the route used by the returning British force.

Tragic Death of a Baby Boy and Other Cannon Mishaps

Today, on the median near the intersection of High and Cross Streets on the northwest end of Monument Park in historic Chestertown, is conspicuously displayed a six-pounder* cast-iron field cannon. An 1899 newspaper report claims that this cannon was one of the four American guns used at the Battle of Caulks Field (see "Captain Parker and His Whiskey-Filled Coffin" for details of this battle).[29]

As was the custom of the time, cannons were often fired as part of celebrations. According to the *Chestertown Spy* newspaper, a cannon was fired in a celebratory mode in Chestertown on July 9, 1793. In 1842, disaster struck early in the morning of July 4 when the gunpowder charges for a celebratory cannon firing blew up prematurely, destroying a store and nearby house. The celebration was cancelled.[30]

The following Fourth of July celebration in 1843 was even worse. This time, the gun was fired, but the Kent Guard who operated the cannon either aimed poorly, loaded too large a charge or did not see a nanny holding the eighteen-month-old son of Mr. Vanhorn. The infant was struck by the cannon wad,* which broke his arm in three places and caused his death the next day.[31] A very similar death caused by a cannon wad is inscribed on the tombstone of Robert

Pre–Revolutionary War cannon reputed to be used during the Battle of Caulks Field. *Ralph Eshelman photograph.*

Morris Sr. at the White Marsh Episcopal Church graveyard near Hambelton, Talbot County. The inscription reads, "A salute from the cannon of a ship the wad fracturing his arm was the signal by which he departed." A second tombstone, in Greensboro Cemetery, Caroline County, is inscribed "SACRED to the memory of Alexander Harrington, who was instantaneously killed by the bursting of a canon [*sic*] on the 4th of July 1835."

Years later, according to an 1899 newspaper, the Chestertown cannon, lying forgotten in the street, was removed, painted and mounted at an unidentified location.[32] More recent research indicates that the cannon was initially placed at the market house, where Fountain Park is located today. It was then moved to a schoolhouse near the intersection of South Cross Street and fittingly named Cannon Street. Apparently after 1899, the cannon was acquired by John S. Vandegrift, the town barber, who embedded it in the ground as a hitching post outside his shop. In 1914, the cannon was acquired by Hopewell Horsey Barroll and used as a lawn ornament on his property on the Chester River. The family donated the cannon to the town as a tribute to Morris Keene Barroll (1893–1962). The plaque on the cannon makes no mention of a young boy having been killed by the gun nor that the cannon had been used in the Battle of Caulks Field.[33]

The cannon at Monument Park is a pre–Revolutionary War gun, and it is known that early cannons were used by the militia* during the War of 1812.

Is it possible that these various newspaper accounts are referring to two different cannons? There were four cannons on the Caulks Field battlefield. At present, it cannot be confirmed that this gun was used at Caulks Field. If this connection could be proven, this cannon would have helped to win not only an American victory at Caulks Field but was twenty-nine years later part of a tragic accident that ended the life of an innocent child. Perhaps because of the association of the cannon to the tragic accident of a child's death, folks wanted to forget—not remember—this cannon.

Sheep and the Battle of St. Paul's Churchyard

Historic St. Paul's Parish is located at the intersection of Sandy Bottom and Ricauds Branch Roads, about six miles southwest of Chestertown. The parish was established in 1692, and the present church structure dates from circa 1713. St. Paul's is among the oldest churches in continuous use in Maryland. The vestry house of St. Paul's has the date 1766 formed with glazed bricks on the north gable end.

Less than two miles to the northwest is Caulks Field, where on August 31, 1814, under a full moon, the British attacked the local militia* (for information on this engagement, see "Captain Parker and His Whiskey-Filled Coffin"). There is a legend that on the church grounds took place the "Battle of St. Paul's Church Yard." The story claims that during the night of August 30 and early morning of August 31, 1814, Lieutenant Colonel Philip Reed, commander of the local militia, moved his men to the St. Paul's Churchyard to rest after the battle at Caulks Field. The legend suggests that most slept in the church to seek protection from the rain while two men were put on sentry duty outside. Well after midnight, one of the sentries, young Jeb Haskins, heard strange noises. Frightened, he sought out the other sentry, Stewart Jacobs, who had also heard noises. They ran into each other, further frightening themselves. Haskins ran to alert Colonel Reed, who feared the British might have snuck up on them. Then a musket sounded. Jacobs had fired in the direction of the noise, believing he had seen a figure. Figures were now appearing all over the churchyard. More muskets were fired. Finally, after several minutes, it was realized that the figures were those of sheep that had wandered into the churchyard.[34]

It is possible that a small contingent of militia was stationed at St. Paul's that night or, perhaps, that some elements of Reed's unit occupied St. Paul's

St. Paul's Churchyard. *Ralph Eshelman photograph.*

after the real battle and were overly jittery from the earlier engagement. It is interesting that specific names are given for the sentries who supposedly were on duty that night, but neither name, Jeb Haskins or Stewart Jacobs, appears in any of the Maryland militia roster lists. Furthermore, none of the contemporary reports indicate that it rained the night of August 30 or early morning of August 31 but state instead that it was a clear, moonlit night. The Battle of St. Paul's Churchyard must be considered a myth and was probably borrowed from some other location and perhaps even a different war.

"The Raising of the Oars" at Worton Creek

On October 18, 1902, during the unveiling of the Caulks Field Monument, the orator of the day, William M. Marine, noted lawyer and author, recounted a story about Worton Creek. The incident supposedly occurred on July 10, 1814, nearly three months before the Battle of Caulks Field (for more information about this engagement, see "Captain Parker and

Sea Scouts provide an impression of "The Raising of the Oars." *Courtesy of http:// wrseascouts.wordpress.com/author/seascouts100.*

His Whiskey-Filled Coffin"). British warships were detected offshore of Kent County. Lieutenant Colonel Philip Reed, commander of the 29th Regiment militia,* responded to this alarm by putting his men on alert and placing lookouts along the shoreline. Following is Marine's story of one British encounter:

> *Just prior to the engagement at Caulks Field, an incident occurred at Worton Creek. The enemy's boats were under heavy fire. [A] shower of ounce balls pierced through the sides of a barge below the water line so that the men in it were placed on the opposite side to keep the bullet [musket ball] holes out of [the] water. The [American musket] fire on them in this situation was so hot that their oars were raised, blade upward, but the Americans kept pegging away until they were lowered. The officer in charge of the boat stood up in the stern sheets and waved his hat until they were safely out of range. Colonel Reed, who had hastened to the*

scene, explained to his men that the raising of the oars, blade up, was the man-of-wars men's method of indicating surrender. They had captured the barge but did not know it.[35]

It is true that the local militia repulsed a British raid on Worton Creek on July 10 (some accounts say June 11), but no contemporary documentation is known to confirm the raising of the oars story.

The Eastern Neck Island Ruse

An Eastern Shore ruse reputedly took place on Eastern Neck Island, today the Eastern Neck National Wildlife Refuge, visible to the north when crossing the Kent Island Narrows Bridge along the Ocean Highway (U.S. Route 50). When the British established their base on Kent Island in August 1814, Lieutenant Colonel Philip Reed, commander of the 21st Regiment of the Maryland Militia, directed his cavalry, a small force, to cross from the mainland at Trumpington Farm to Eastern Neck Island in full view of the British lookout-boats stationed at the mouth of Chester River. By countermarching and continually recrossing the river in a ferry scow,* the Americans hoped to fool the British into believing that they had a much larger force than they really did.

This legend dates from remarks given beside the grave of Lieutenant General Reed at I.U. Church, Kent County, Maryland, on September 13, 1959, during a reunion picnic. There are no known documents to support the ruse, if it did occur, it may have worked because Captain Peter Parker, commander of a British squadron in the upper Chesapeake Bay, was "running down the Eastern shore of Maryland on [August] the 27th. I was surprised to observe the enemy's regular troops and militia in motion along the whole coast."[36]

Kitty Knight: Heroine on the Sassafras

Georgetown lies on the south side of the Sassafras River overlooking the adjacent village of Fredericktown in Cecil County. On a hill above the river at Georgetown are two late-eighteenth-century houses that survived

Kitty Knight pleads with Admiral Cockburn to spare her house while Fredericktown and Georgetown are in flames. © *Gerry Embleton illustration.*

the devastation brought on by the British during a raid on the twin towns on May 28, 1813. The British were furious that the Americans had fired upon them after having warned them to remain peacefully in their homes. To teach the resisters a lesson, the raiders burned homes, businesses and granaries, but two prominent brick homes on the hill were saved by the efforts of heroine Catherine "Kitty" Knight (c. 1775–1855), the daughter of John and Catherine Knight, prominent village citizens.

On the north side of the river at Fredericktown, ten dwellings, three granaries and a storehouse were destroyed. On the south side at Georgetown, thirteen dwellings, stables and outbuildings were destroyed, as well as a cobbler's shop, tavern, granary and storehouse. After ransacking and burning these targets, the British marauders proceeded quickly up the hill toward the two brick homes, one in which Kitty Knight lived. Rear Admiral George Cockburn and his Royal Marines had already put the torch to one of these houses, which was occupied by a sick and destitute old woman. Miss Kitty pleaded for the old woman's home and managed to convince the admiral not to burn the house. Miss Kitty is reported to have stamped out the flames herself. The raiders then approached Kitty's home, but her pleas were sufficient for Cockburn to end the destruction. They had by this time destroyed most of the two towns. The lesson has been taught—enough was enough.

The first known written documentation of this legendary heroic act was in a local newspaper dated November 22, 1855, in an article reporting Miss Kitty Knight's recent death. It reads, "By her heroism at the burning of Georgetown…she saved several families from being made homeless and friendless by the fire and sword."[37] The article claims that her appeal and possibly her charm so moved the admiral that he ordered the troops to their barges and left unburned a church and several remaining houses. There is no contemporary documentation to support this legend other than the obituary, written forty-two years after the actual event. Although the legend may have been embellished, there appears to be at least some kernel of truth to it.

In 1836, Kitty Knight bought the house she had been renting and remained there until her death in 1855. As she requested, Kitty's tombstone is inscribed simply "Miss Catherine Knight," having never married. Both houses she saved have been incorporated into the Kitty Knight Inn. Kitty is buried nearby in the Old Bohemia churchyard of St. Francis Xavier Shrine in Cecil County. Her tombstone reads in full:

A maiden fair, with courage bold
With spirit pure and high,
Displayed her flag of truce, and all
For poor humanity.
SACRED / *To the memory of* MISS CATHERINE KNIGHT, *who departed*
this life on the 22d day of November 1855 in the 79ᵗʰ year of her age.

QUEEN ANNE'S COUNTY

Tory Secret Dinners with the British

On February 1, 1900, Mrs. Mary Elizabeth Thomas, born 1802, died at her home in Quaker Neck at the age of ninety-eight. Although she was only a child of ten at the time, she claimed to remember several events from the War of 1812. One was that British naval officer Captain Sir Peter Parker of HM frigate* *Menelaus* and several of his officers "were frequent visitors" at her parents' (James and Henrietta Hart) home at Queenstown, where she was born. Her obituary states:

> *She remembered they always came at night, as the American soldiers were near Queenstown ready to give battle. The British frequently partook of substantial midnight suppers at the Hart home. Her father it may be understood was a Tory and at one time fed 100 of the British soldiers.*[38]

The *Menelaus* never ventured into the Chester River during the war but did visit the upper eastern shore of Kent County in late August 1814. Queenstown was the site of a pre-dawn British attack and skirmish on August 13, 1813, but Parker was not part of that attack. It seems that Mrs. Thomas has confused the Battle of Caulks Field event of 1814 with the Queenstown event of 1813. It is very unlikely that British officers could have had secret dinners with a Tory, let alone to one hundred soldiers. This is more likely a tale she was told as a child that had become distorted over time and repeated in later years based on faulty memory.

The obituary also states that she remembered with "peculiar distinctness" the arrest of a Mr. Mitchell, who was a deserter from the English army and "still owed three years in the service." There were several British deserters, but none to our knowledge was named Mitchell. Again, here is a scrambling of the facts. The arrest was probably that of Joseph Mitchell, who was the regimental quartermaster for the 21st Maryland Regiment, Kent County, on September 5, 1814. Mitchell was taken onboard the *Menelaus*, placed in prison and not released until after the war. He was not a British deserter (see "The Mitchell House and Parker's Blanket").

This obituary is an example of the jumbling of facts. Did Mrs. Thomas incorrectly remember the stories her parents had told her over the years? Did the person who supplied the information to the newspaper correctly remember the stories that Mrs. Thomas had told over the years and/or did the newspaper correctly publish what was given to them? Regardless, we know the facts are misconstrued. The stories of secret dinners and a deserter are probably family tales told to Mary Elizabeth as a child and/or a tale she told her children that had been embellished over time.

SOMERSET COUNTY

The Big Annemessex River Stick Gun Ruse

On May 19, 1814, a British vessel came into the Big Annemessex River, located between Manokin River to the north and Little Annemessex River (Crisfield) to the south. In the early morning, a British raiding party boarded an anchored vessel belonging to George Davey and set it on fire. Captain Davey was awakened in his home by the commotion and quickly assembled enough men to man four log canoes* to attack the raiding party. Davey also ordered "the negroes [to] march down opposite to them [British], with sticks shouldered as guns." The ruse, if true, might have been successful, as a warning cannon shot from HM brig-sloop *Jaseur* alerted the British marauders of the approaching canoes. The Big Annemessex River raid, published in the local newspaper only days after the event, is reprinted here:

Captain Davey immediately manned and sent off four canoe, the men in the canoes would have captured or had a brush with them had not

1890 drawing of a Chesapeake log canoe suggesting what a canoe might have looked like in 1814. Taken from 1890 U.S. Fish Commission report.

> *the alarm gun have been fired from the Jasseur [sic], upon which they, the British, rowed off, though so without receiving a salute from the men on board the canoes, as well as the militia* who were collecting; Or, as others say, that Capt. Davey had that presence of mind to make the negroes march down opposite to them, with sticks shouldered as guns—the vessels not much injured.*[39]

This legend is one that actually has a source written within days of the event. While this does not prove the legend, it does give it more credibility. The ruse of using sticks to look like guns is similar to the Mount Ephraim ruse (see "The Corn Stalk Ruse at Mount Ephraim"), in which corn stalks were reputedly used for the same purpose. But that legend has no contemporary record to support the claim, as does the Big Annemessex River stick gun ruse.

TALBOT COUNTY

Jacob Gibson's Ruse

In 1810, Jacob Gibson purchased Sharps Island at the mouth of the Choptank River, about fifteen miles from St. Michaels. Gibson was a farmer, politician, banker, eccentric and one of the most controversial personalities in Talbot County at the time. On April 12, 1813, the British raided Sharps Island, confiscating Gibson's livestock and holding him prisoner. As was usually the custom, the British left $54 in cash and a bill to their government to pay later the remainder of the $225, which they determined was a fair market value for the four sheep, twelve cattle and twenty-eight hogs they took. However, Gibson was later accused of having been given "a very extravagant price for what they took." In fact, what Gibson was paid was below the fair market value. Still, to stem the protests and possibly out of fear of being accused a traitor, Gibson donated the money he received for his losses to the government. But Gibson was nevertheless accused of collusion with the dreaded enemy.[40]

On the morning of April 18, a detachment of Captain Robert Banning's Patriotic Blues Troop of Horse sighted what appeared to be an enemy vessel approaching St. Michaels from the south. From town, they saw what they believed to be a Union Jack flying from the mast and heard the sounds of a beating drum. Women and children were sent into the countryside to get them out of harms way while the militia* were hastily assembled. As the craft got closer, it was soon discovered not to be a British vessel but a local boat commanded by Captain Jacob Gibson. Gibson had purposely disguised his vessel with a red bandana tied to its masthead, and the drum sounds were emanating from a ragged negro boy beating the head of an empty rum barrel.

Upon learning of the prank, the town's citizens became furious, and legend claims that Gibson donated two cannons to the town as a peace offering.[41] It is not certain, but these guns may have been used to help defend the town during subsequent attacks by the British in August of that same year. After the war, the cannons were placed at the Easton Arsenal, where they were confiscated in May 1861 by Federal troops from Baltimore during the Civil War to keep them from possible use by Southern sympathizers.

Replica War of 1812 cannons serve as a memorial to two original cannons donated in 1813 by prankster Jacob Gibson. *Ralph Eshelman photograph.*

The confiscated cannons were taken to Baltimore and are believed to have been stored at Fort McHenry. In 1964, residents of St. Michaels claimed that these two cannons were rightfully the property of the town and demanded their return from the National Park Service, which then administered the fort. The debate continued until the National Park Service presented the town with the two replica six-pounder* cannons, which were mounted in 1974 at Muskrat Park, formally known as Church Cove Park, at the foot of Green Street as a reminder of the 1813 incident.

While embellished, this legend is based on fact because Gibson himself wrote a letter to Secretary of State James Monroe and Maryland governor Levin Winder on April 24, 1813, and his letter was later published in the local newspapers. Gibson's frolic with the citizens of St. Michaels was only a hoax in poor taste, but it did help prepare the citizens for what was yet to come.

The Town That Fooled the British

St. Michaels became known as "The Town That Fooled the British" by placing lanterns in trees and on ship masts to cause the British to overshoot the town during a morning cannonade.* This story began with one of St. Michaels' favorite sons, Thomas Kemp Jr. (1800–1890), a thirteen-year-old boy at the time of the 1813 British attack. Seventy-three years later, during an 1886 interview for the *Baltimore American* newspaper, Kemp stated, "Lights were placed at night upon trees and masts of vessels." His father, Captain Joseph Kemp, had commanded the St. Michaels Patriotic Blues, which garrisoned a small cannon battery during the 1813 attack.[42]

In 1898, Prentiss E. Ingraham's *Land of Legendary Lore: Sketches of Romance and Reality on the Eastern Shore of the Chesapeake* was the first to briefly recount the story in book form—thus, along with the newspaper article, the story of the "lanterns in the trees" became established.[43] The story was renewed by Thomas H. Sewall in his 1913 article "The Battle of St. Michael's, 1813–1814," published in the *Baltimore American* during the centennial celebration of the War of 1812. Sewall wrote, "To deceive the enemy, the citizens had placed lights in the tops of the tallest trees and houses."[44]

Fifty years later, in 1963, during the 150th anniversary of the battle, Gilbert Bryon, a popular Maryland author, recounted the story in his *St. Michaels: The Town that Fooled the British; A Complete Account of the British Attacks on St.*

Young boys hang lanterns in trees and from ship masts in the harbor to fool British gunners. *Courtesy of artist Robert Papp.*

Michaels during the War of 1812. In it, Bryon states, "After the British marines retreated to their boats, the gunners trained their cannon on the town. But the misty lights in the tree tops misdirected their fire, and the British overshot the town." The booklet remains a favorite local chronicle.[45]

In 1995, Norman H. Plummer investigated the lore surrounding the lantern story using archival resources unavailable to Sewall and Bryon.[46] Plummer determined that by the time of the cannonade on the town, dawn had already appeared at 5:09 a.m. Furthermore, none of the contemporary military reports or newspaper accounts refer to any lanterns having been placed in trees, ships or tall buildings to fool the British. Plummer concluded that the entire story was derived from the memory of a then eighty-six-year-old man recounting what he claimed to remember from when he was a thirteen-year-old boy. Even if the citizens had hung lanterns in the trees, they did not "fool" the British. General Perry Benson, who had commanded the American militia during the attack, stated that many of the "houses were perforated" by cannonballs during the cannonade. The famous Cannonball House, touted as one of the homes hit by the British during the cannonade, lends credence to Benson's statement. Still, the account of the Cannonball House first appeared in 1907 from William Fairbanks, an elderly man, nearly a century after the event.[47] Why was there no earlier mention of this specific house having been hit by a cannonball?

Humorist Rick Kollinger claims that the story was fabricated to boost tourism and that in effect, St. Michaels is the town that fools the tourist, not the British.[48] Other townsfolk could find humor in the story and tell tales of how Mr. Pastorfield, one of the defenders, ran so fast that he tripped and fell in his hog pen, and when one of his hogs nudged him, he cried out, "I surrender! I surrender!" William Caulk jumped into his boat and rowed all night long out to the British squadron to surrender, calling, "I'm coming, Mr. British! I'm coming!" not realizing that in his panic he had forgotten to untie his boat.[49]

Finally, the British attack was a surprise attack. The American defenders did not detect the enemy assault until the last minute. How did the villagers have time to hang lanterns? How did the citizens of St. Michaels know the British were going to cannonade the town? The story of the "lanterns in the trees" and St. Michael's proclaiming that it is "The Town That Fooled the British" must be placed in the category of popular lore from the War of 1812. Yet this has failed to stem the many popular articles and children's books written about this myth—which may not be such a bad thing.

The Royal Oak Cannonballs

One of the most enduring legends of the War of 1812 on Maryland's Eastern Shore concerns two War of 1812 cannonballs that once hung from a limb of an old oak tree four miles from St. Michaels. The oak tree, originally known as "Bartlett's Oak" but better known as the "Royal Oak," was described as "a venerable monarch of the forest, huge and wide spreading, and from those limbs above the roadway hung two cannon balls."[50] At one foot above the ground, the white oak had a circumference of forty feet and a diameter of nine feet. The grand tree was said to have stood during the days of the American Revolution and served as a rendezvous site for the minutemen of 1776.[51] In 1812, Captain Thomas Wayman's militia* company, "Hearts of Oak," assembled here, just as their fathers had thirty-seven years before.

Legend claims that following the Battle of St. Michaels in August 1813, Captain Robert Banning (1776–1845) of the St. Michael's militia company Patriotic Blues retrieved two British cannonballs that had been fired on the town and hung them with iron straps from one of the massive limbs of the oak.[52]

In July 1858, the Royal Oak, "from old age and the heat of the summer's sun, withered and died."[53] In 1867, the dead tree was cut down by T.D. Pastorfield due to fear it would fall onto passersby traveling under its sweeping rotten limbs. Soon after its demise, the *Easton Gazette* printed the following poem written by a woman known simply as "Emily."

Royal Oak cannonball and grapeshot. *Ralph Eshelman photograph.*

The wind sends forth a wail,
From the woodland depths around,
Where the green leaves shiver dewy tears,
As the monarch tree of untold years,
Stands, with ring on the ground!

It, stood, a sentinel,
Watching ages depart,
It look'd on the first hamlet's smoke,
And heard the death-knell of each oak,
As the axe struck its heart!

Could'st thou not spare us, time,
One of the relics hoar,
Which had known ancestral birth and death,
And towered sublime ere the first breath,
Of Freedom swept our shore?

Mighty, in ruin laid!
What scenes hast thou not known,
When light, wild foot-steps track'd each maze,
In the far misty forest days,
Of races long since gone!

Ah! Could the old oak tell,
The wonders of its lore,
How would its buried legends sway,
The wisest children of to-day,
With histories of yore!

A sacred mem'ry long,
Shall linger o'er its rest;
Emotion fill each patriot heart,
As fair rememberance with true art,
Paints with proud verdant crest.

Our patriarch of the soil,
With calm defiant air,
That caught two war-tide's fiery rain,
And in grim mock'ry held in chain,
Till death, the LEAD FRUIT THERE![54]

Where did the cannonballs come from? One 1858 account claims that the Royal Oak was "pierced in both conflicts" of the Revolutionary War and the War of 1812. It suggests that one cannonball from each war made up the two balls that hung on the oak.[55] An 1884 account claims that one of the cannonballs was a "twenty-pounder"* found the day after the British cannonade* of St. Michaels on August 10, 1813. The other ball was grapeshot,* supposedly from the same action.[56] Since the oak tree was located four miles away at Royal Oak and far beyond the range of the English cannon, we know that the great tree was not hit during the St. Michaels engagement.

One of the more interesting versions of this story is that the twenty-pound cannonball destroyed a chicken coop in St. Michaels on the morning of the cannonade,* killing three chickens, the only American losses in the battle.[57]

Who hung the cannonballs from the Royal Oak? For years, George McKinstry, the town's factotum, served as blacksmith, gunsmith, wheelwright and miller, and it very well may have been him who banded the two balls together with an iron strap in order to hang them from one of the oak tree's massive limbs.[58]

The hanging cannonballs eventually made it into the hands of a local Miles River oysterman named Elijah Marshall, who used them as an anchor for his boat. This was probably after the old tree had died and certainly before—or when—the limbs were cut down in 1867. Henry G. Banning recognized the significance of the cannonballs and somehow obtained ownership and took them to his home in Wilmington, Delaware.[59] In 1885, he returned the cannonballs to the town in the custody of a Dr. Robinson, who installed them in an honored place upon a locust tree in front of Mr. Pastorfield's drugstore that stood near the famous stump of the Royal Oak.[60] Oak Creek Sales, an antique store, occupies the site today. While the origin and details of the story of the cannonballs cannot be confirmed, the cannonballs themselves are displayed today inside the Royal Oak Post Office. As can be seen in the photograph above, one is indeed a cannonball and the other a grapeshot,* both probably from the British attack on St. Michaels in August 1813.[61] It does seem odd that a militia* company called the St. Michaels Patriotic Blues sought the souvenir balls and hung them in the great oak tree rather than the Hearts of Oak company that used the tree as an assembly point. Could the legend be wrong?

Carolinians Mistake the Talbot Militia for the British

This tale was a good-natured jibe between the militiamen* of Caroline and Talbot Counties. It supposedly took place in 1813 when the British were marauding around Talbot County (see "The Town That Fooled the British"). Here, this humorous but obviously fabricated story is told as published, as one huge paragraph, in an 1861 letter to the editor of the *Easton Star* newspaper.

> *The gallant people beyond the bridge of Dover* [over the Choptank River that separates Talbot and Caroline Counties], *had raided a company which generously offered its services for frontier defense, they having nothing to apprehend in their interior fastnesses, from the marauders of watermelon patches and the robbers of hen-roosts and milk houses. This company fully accoutered in the arms and equipage peculiar to the interior, with cornstalk bayonets bristling like the hirsute appendage on a mad boar's back and*

whiskers well pomatamed [sic] *with the butt end of an oppossum's* [sic] *tail in lieu of a candle, crossed the bridge and were in rapid march to join their fellow soldiers at Fort Stokes when their approach was announced at Easton. There were at that time two companies of Infantry belonging to Easton; one which had marched to the seat of war at St. Michaels. The other, the "Fencibles,"* commanded by Captain, afterwards Colonel K___* [Kemp], *with all the urbanity for which Eastonians are well known, upon hearing of the coming of their noble-hearted auxiliaries, went on their way to meet and escort them into town. The bellicose demonstrations of the Easton warriors, however, were too much for the unpracticed gallantry of the magnanimous Carolinians, and mistaking the intended escort for the enemies of the nation, with a prudence unsurpassed by anything except their benignity in offering their services, took the back track for home, thinking it decidedly more glorious sport to catch herrings in the Spring-time, than to perish amid the horrors and the havoc of the battle field, even though when dying they might be cheered by the consolation that it was for their country. It was fortunate for the country that the draw was up when they again reached the bridge, as it checked their homeward progress; or it is likely history would not have had the happiness to record their subsequent deed of valour* [sic]. *They were caught on the bridge by the Eastonians, harangued in a very polite address by Capt. K___, persuaded by the eloquence for which he was so justly distinguished, that the "Fencibles," though they did exhibit their military capabilities in smart waistcoats, burnished boots, and ruffled shirts were not enemies but genuine friends who would treat them hospitably at Fort Stokes and indoctrinate them into the mysteries of roasting and eating certain animals like the crustaceous and molusk* [sic] *families, to them, natural curiosities called crabs and oysters. Overwhelmed by the power of such artillery as this, the strangers surrendered at discretion and were conducted in triumph to the Fort. It was reported that they became the most vigilant of guards, keeping watch night and day—never daring to venture outside the breastworks for fear of stumbling over the enemies in the bushes, and with eyes raised just above the counterscarp, looking intently down the river or peering cautiously through the embrasure in dread of an approaching foe.*[62]

What makes this humorous story even more interesting is that the following year (1862), during the middle of the Civil War, a similar story appeared in the same newspaper, but this time it was mistaken Union troops rather than mistaken British troops:

Alas! That Cow Landing, the heroic city that defied the British in 1812 and preserved her honor untarnished throughout that trying war, should now ignominiously have to succumb to a squad of Caroline sand diggers. This would not have been if the immortal Governor of the city had been present on the fatal day, with his poplar log artillery [fake cannon], *buck horns, and regimentals. Do send us some arms for defense— toothpicks, if you have nothing else that we may wipe out the digrace* [sic], *COW LANDING.*[63]

It is clear from the sarcasm and humor that the writer did not intend to mislead readers, only to entertain them. (For a similarly entertaining Virginia tale, see "Cross-eyed Rooster Thief.")

WORCESTER COUNTY

The Corn Stalk Ruse at Mount Ephraim

Mount Ephraim, located along Bayside Road, south of Public Landing and overlooking Chincoteague Bay, was built circa 1770. Littleton Robin Prunell, while staying at Mount Ephraim, is reputed to have noticed several suspicious ships approaching Chincoteague Bay. Believing them to be British warships coming to raid the area, he assembled men, women and children from the farm, built a fire and marched them around the barn with corn stalks over their shoulders while he led them on a white horse. According to this tale, their actions caused the British to believe that the local militia* were conducting military drills near their campfire, forcing them to seek a less defended area to raid.

Another version of this incident holds that the British first bombarded the farm and then landed in search of supplies, during which they set fire to the kitchen floor. A kettle in which flax was being boiled was upset to put out the fire, and a charred section of the floor remains to this day. Other sources claim that this event occurred during the Revolutionary War, while yet another legend claims that the same ruse was used to ward off pirates from Mount Ephraim.[64] This corn stalk ruse is similar to the stick gun ruse said to have been used at Big Annemessex River in Somerset County, Maryland.

Children playing at Mount Ephraim. *D.H. Smith 1940 photograph, Library of Congress.*

It is probable that this legend is a combination of other legends from Worcester County. Henry's Grove, Genesar, and Fassitt House, eighteenth-century brick structures facing Sinepuxent Bay, are said to have been fired upon by the British either during the American Revolutionary War or the War of 1812. The Fassitt House legend goes even further, claiming that the inhabitants, fearing a British raid, buried their family silver only to forget the hiding place. Hopeful treasure-seekers dug holes around the house in search of the silver, but it has never been found.[65] Thus far, there is no primary documentation to substantiate any of these claims.

Maryland Western Shore

How Did Fort Nonsense Get Its Name?

Protected by four forts, Annapolis was the most fortified city in Maryland at the beginning of the War of 1812. Fort Severn was located on the grounds of what today is the U.S. Naval Academy. Just to the south at East Port was Fort Horn at Horn Point. On the opposite side of the Severn River, where the David Taylor Naval Ship Research and Development Center is located today, were Fort Madison and Fort Nonsense. All the forts were built along the water to protect the capital city from possible naval attack—all except Fort Nonsense. This fort was built on the highest ground overlooking Fort Madison and the Severn River. Legends claim that the fort got its name because it did not make sense to construct a fort out of gun range to protect the river and the city of Annapolis. On the site of Fort Nonsense is a plaque that reads:

> *Fort Nonsense has been placed on the National Register of Historic Places by the U.S. Department of the Interior. It is the last remaining fortification of several constructed in the 18th and early 19th centuries to defend Annapolis*

Fort Nonsense earthworks* are still discernible among the trees overlooking the Severn River. *Ralph Eshelman photograph.*

and its waterways. It is a "Redoubt" or small, independent earthen site. Its origin and unusual name are a mystery, but records show it was built in the early 19th century. It may have been a lookout point for Fort Madison, a masonry structure along the banks of the Severn River. There is no record of combat at Fort Nonsense or at any of the Annapolis forts.

An 1844 U.S. Army Corps of Engineers report mentions "old Fort Nonsense" and states that it was built to deter an attack from the rear of Fort Madison less than a half mile away.[66] Therefore, Fort Nonsense was not a foolish and unnecessary government boondoggle. Due to its military purpose, the fort made sense and could more appropriately be called "Fort Makes Sense."

BALTIMORE CITY

Did General Lingan Die During the Baltimore Riots or Escape to Canada?

Americans were sharply divided over the War of 1812. When the *Baltimore Federal Republican* newspaper published an editorial against the war, an angry mob of several hundred Democratic-Republicans destroyed the newspaper's office building and its contents on the evening of June 22, 1812, only four days after war had been declared. When the Federalist newspaper reopened a month later at a second location in Baltimore, a mob of Democratic-

Republicans surrounded the office on July 27. But this time the building was defended by fifty armed Federalists, including General Henry "Light Horse Harry" Lee, father of Robert E. Lee. The besieged Federalists fired a warning burst that first scattered the mob, but when the crowd, estimated to number about one thousand, again formed and pushed through the house doorway, the occupants opened fire, killing one and wounding several more. The mob threatened to fire a cannon loaded with grapeshot* into the building. Finally, city officials arrived and persuaded some twenty-five Federalists to surrender to protective custody and took them to the safety of the jail. On the way, paving stones were hurled at the Federalists, hitting one in the face and almost knocking another down.

During the night of July 28, the Democratic-Republican mob stormed the jail and beat and stabbed nine of the Federalist sympathizers as city officials stood by. One Federalist was stripped, tarred, feathered, dumped in a cart and clubbed as rioters pulled him through the city. At one point, his feathers were set on fire. Women in the crowd reportedly chanted, "Kill the Tories." General Lee, who had eulogized George Washington, lost one eye while being beaten into a limp and bloody mess. He never fully recovered from his injuries. Brigadier General James McCubbin Lingan, age sixty, died several hours after having been beaten and stabbed in the chest despite his pleas for mercy.

Many Baltimoreans were outraged by the incident. A memorial broadside to the memory of General Lingan was printed and circulated. George Washington Custis eulogized Lingan saying, "Oh Maryland! Would that waters of the Chesapeake could wash this foul stain from thy character!" Lingan was buried in Georgetown, and on November 5, 1908, his remains were reinterred in Arlington National Cemetery in Virginia.

Baltimoreans were sharply divided over the war, resulting in riots and even the death of General Lingan. © *Gerry Embleton illustration.*

James Darling, a participant of the Baltimore Riot, later told a story that General Lingan had not died in the riot and had escaped to Canada. The story was retold to Mr. J.W. Smith and was eventually published in a Baltimore newspaper in 1905. Smith claimed the incident was a case of mistaken identity and that, in the darkness of the night, the men who attacked the Federalists believed they had killed Lingan but that the body turned out to be that of a man who had been imprisoned for debt. Friends of Lingan "furnished disguises and gave him enough money to flee the country."[67]

Another report of mistaken identity surfaced after the Great Baltimore Fire of 1904 when laborers razed one of the buildings and found skeletal remains inside a room with a window protected by iron bars. A Mr. Mackenzie said he believed "the old house was a center during the riots of July 27–28, 1812, which culminated in the killing of Gen. James. M. Lingan…one of the rooms of the house had iron bars and gave every evidence of it once having been used as a prison room."[68] This amazing story passed through three generations but was not published until 1905, eighty-two years after the event. The 1812 Baltimore Riots were used to explain the discovery of skeletons found in a room with iron bars on a window. It is well known that the mob stormed a jail, but that jail is believed to have been located at Buren and Madison Streets, the current site of the Maryland State Penitentiary, not at "Charles and Raidersion" [misspelling of Madison?] Streets as indicated in the newspaper article. This is an example of how a legend can be used to rationalize a situation that has no known explanation. Would the city officials have allowed the body of General Lingan—or even the body of a debtor—to decay inside one of its jail cells?

A full investigation was conducted by the Maryland House of Delegates after the riots, and no mention was made of mistaken identification. All accounts indicate that Lingan was killed by the mob. There are three instances in the 364-page report in which there is a slight suggestion of possible doubt, but not enough to support the story that Lingan did not die in the jail.[69] This story must be considered a myth.

Nest of Pirates

The phrase "nest of pirates" goes back at least to the days of the American Revolution (1782), with "that infernal nest of pirates at Providence." It reappears with the Dey of Algiers (1804) of the Barbary Coast: "That

Baltimore privateer *Vigilant. Courtesy of Maryland Historical Society.*

Algiers, the nest of pirates who have with impunity, for many years past, declared war against the property of the whole mercantile world."[70] Also, British Vice Admiral Alexander Cochrane ordered a squadron to Tortola, West Indies, in July 1806 "to destroy the shipping and burn the town, in order to root out that nest of pirates, and privateersmen."[71]

In 1808, a Boston newspaper proclaimed, "The land of our fathers, whence is derived the best blood of our nation, the country to which we are chiefly indebted for our laws and knowledge, is stigmatized as a nest of pirates, plunderers and assassins."[72]

Jean Lafitte of the Barataria region of the Gulf of Mexico was one of the best-known and most legendary pirates during the War of 1812. He preyed upon merchant vessels but redeemed himself when he and his men assisted in the defense of New Orleans in 1814–15.[73]

The phrase "nest of pirates" has also been attributed to Baltimore because of the number of privateers who built and operated there during the War of 1812. Where are the sources to make such a claim? After looking at contemporary newspapers and military reports, we could find no reference to

Baltimore as a "nest of pirates." The origin of this phrase used in connection with Baltimore came not from the British but apparently from Maryland historian John Thomas Scharf (1843–1898), who gave a lecture at Baltimore's Schuetzen Verin (shooting club) Park in October 1880. Scharf stated:

> *Great Britain's power in defense of State autonomy and in defense of seamen's rights transformed this busy little seaport into a "nest of pirates," which sent out its wasps to sting British commerce on every sea.*[74]

John Thomas Scharf, again in 1881, refers to a nest of pirates when he stated, "In the Revolutionary War, the English government regarded the Chesapeake Bay as a nest of pirates."[75]

Ironically, the only contemporary reference we could find of the use of pirates in connection with the Chesapeake during the War of 1812 does not refer to Baltimore at all but instead to the British themselves. A Pennsylvania newspaper, the *Carlisle Gazette*, titled an article on the British attack on Queenstown, Maryland, in August 1813 as "The Pirates of the Chesapeake."[76]

Perhaps the most interesting account comes from the *Niles' Weekly Register* in 1811:

> *Mr. Lindsey is requested by one of his subscribers to insert in his paper, that the doctor of the privateer Saratoga (now fitting for a cruise at Fairhaven) applied some days since, to several apothecaries of this place for a medicine chest; all of whom peremptorily refused supplying him with that article, or with any drugs or medicines for the use of the privateer.*
>
> *We think the gentlemen did themselves much credit; and we hope their example will be followed by the citizens of this place generally. Let it be distinctly understood that privateers cannot obtain supplies of any kind at this place, and we shall no longer be infested with those nuisances. Let them fit and refit from that sink of corruption, that Sodom of our country called Baltimore, and not by seeking refuge here, put in jeopardy our shipping and our town, and necessitate our yeomanry at this busy season to leave their farms uncultivated to defend our harbor, which were it not a place of refuge for what has been emphatically denominated "licensed pirates," would not need a soldier to insure its safety—A Ship Owner.*[77]

It was not the British calling Baltimore a haven of "licensed pirates" but a Yankee from Massachusetts. Unless someone can come up with a War of 1812 account of the British calling Baltimore a "nest of pirates," we must consider this claim false. Ironically, the only contemporary account we found claims that it was an American calling the British "pirates" because of their actions in the Chesapeake or a fellow American (Yankee) calling Baltimore a "sink of corruption" for harboring licensed pirates. In 1881, about a hundred years after the American Revolution, it was Scharf who claimed that the British regarded the Chesapeake Bay—not Baltimore—as a nest of pirates. This is a good example of a phrase being repeated over and over until it is considered fact.

Everything They Could Desire

Lieutenant Colonel Joseph Sterett (1771–1821), commander of the 5th Maryland Regiment of Baltimore City, lived at Surrey (formerly Mount Deposit), his estate on Wilbur Avenue, within two miles of the American defenses on Hampstead Hill during the Battle for Baltimore in September 1814.[78] In 1888, his daughter, Mrs. Louisa Sterett Hollins (1816–89), told a story about the British occupying the house. At midnight on September 12, Sterett and his regiment had returned to Baltimore from the Battle at North Point, and early the next morning, he removed his family to Baltimore out of concern for their safety. Sterett took his post on Hampstead Hill, within sight of his estate.

Later that morning, Colonel Arthur Brooke, commander of the British land troops after Major General Robert Ross had been killed (see "General Ross's Last Breath"), supposedly established his field headquarters at the nearby home of William Bowley, called Furley Hall (no longer extant), located near present-day Herring Run Park. About four thousand British troops occupied this area in anticipation of an attack on Baltimore. British officers reportedly helped themselves to Bowley's wine. Some soldiers also entered Sterett's house and removed candles, silver and other domestic items.[79] While here, officers supposedly left the following inscription on the parlor mantel: "Capts. Brown, Wilcocks and McNamara of the Light Brigade, Royal Marines, met with everything they could wish for at this house. They return their thanks, notwithstanding it was received at the hands of the butler in the absence of the colonel."[80]

Louisa Sterett Hollins would have been seventy-two years old in 1888 and her Surrey story a seventy-four-year-old tale, probably told over and over by family members. How much this story may have been embellished over time

Surrey, rebuilt following a fire in the 1920s, was the home of Lieutenant Colonel Joseph Sterett wherein British soldiers enjoyed his wine. *Ralph Eshelman photograph.*

is unclear. Certainly, British officers and troops would have taken advantage by seeking shelter from the miserable rainy conditions. Some wine or other refreshments would have been very welcome, but for officers to have left their names, risking punishment for looting, seems unlikely.

Ode to a Rooster

The origin of the rooster legend during the bombardment* of Fort McHenry was first published in the *Baltimore Patriot* on November 24, 1814, nearly two months after the attack on the fort. Titled "Ode to a Rooster," the article reported that a pet rooster had been struck with shrapnel and from alarm or pain flew up onto the parapet or, as a later report proclaims, to the flagstaff itself, and cock-a-doodle-dooed in defiance:

> [During the bombardment] *a man* [Henry Barnhart], *who was severely indisposed and worn down with fatigue, declared that if he ever lived*

Rooster crows defiantly from the ramparts of Fort McHenry. © *Gerry Embleton illustration.*

to see Baltimore, the young rooster should be treated with pound cake. Not being able to leave the fort, the day after the bombardment he sent to the city, procured the cake, and had fine sport in treating his favorite Rooster.[81]

Niles' Weekly Register reported a nearly identical story in 1815:

During the bombardment of Fort McHenry, at a time when the explosions were the most tremendous, a rooster mounted a parapet and crowed heartily. This excited their laughter and animated the feelings of all present. A man, who was severely indisposed and worn down with fatigue and sickness, declared that if ever he lived to see Baltimore, the rooster should be treated with pound cake. Not being able to leave the fort, the day after the bombardment he sent to the city, procured the cake, and had fine sport in treating his favorite rooster.[82]

The account surfaced again in Colonel John Thomas Scharf's 1874 history of Baltimore, and an identical account was given in the *New York Times* in 1911.[83] In 1932, the *Baltimore Evening Sun* retold the story during the annual anniversary celebration of Defenders' Day, commemorating the Battle for Baltimore. For the first time, the owner of the rooster was identified as Henry Barnhart (1786–1873), who had served during the bombardment. Major George Armistead, commander of the fort, stated that Barnhart "had a chicken cock that he prized very highly…a fragment of a bursting shell, which struck the rooster on his foot, causing it, from alarm or pain to fly up to and light upon the flagstaff."[84]

The legend of a rooster being fed cake at Fort McHenry is considered questionable but possibly true. In the early nineteenth century, barnyard fowl were commonly found at urban military posts. Henry Barnhart did serve as a private in Captain William H. Addison's U.S. Sea Fencibles* at the fort, and soon afterward, Lieutenant Henry Fisher of the 27th Maryland Regiment drew a detailed sketch of the bombardment scene. On the ramparts of the fort just above the gate, in larger-than-life size, he depicts the rooster.[85] Whether the rooster was actually wounded by shrapnel is hard to tell. One version claims that when the rooster died, it was given a full military funeral and buried in a cigar box at the fort. If one day the remains of this rooster are discovered, such a find would add credence to the legend.

But there is a concern. A similar rooster story is told shortly after the naval engagement on Lake Champlain, also fought in September of 1814. During the battle, a British shot reportedly bounced across the deck of the American brig* *Saratoga* and smashed a wooden poultry cage, freeing a gamecock. The indignant rooster took wing and landed in the rigging. Facing the British warships, the cock defiantly called out a challenge to battle.[86] The ship's crew considered this "a propitious omen" to an American victory. It is possible that a rooster was present at both events. The legends of fowl in battle go back to at least the Roman period, when sacred chickens were kept onboard ships to predict the outcome of battles. Before a battle, chickens were fed grain. If the fowl ate the grain, victory was predicted. It was therefore advantageous to keep the chickens hungry, so we can only wonder how well these sacred chickens were fed. The chicken onboard *Saratoga* may have been a source of food or perhaps a good luck pet, as in the Roman tradition. Interestingly, Barnhart was a member of the Sea Fencibles and had a naval background, so perhaps he was perpetuating a naval tradition at Fort McHenry.

Who Published Francis Scott Key's Lyrics?

Everyone knows that Francis Scott Key wrote the words (actually song lyrics) that became the United States national anthem in 1931. But who was responsible for getting Key's lyrics to a printer so they could be read by the public? The first printing of these lyrics was in the form of a broadside issued on September 17, 1814, the day after Key returned to Baltimore. The lyrics first appeared in the *Baltimore Patriot* newspaper three days later on September 20. Key himself never wrote about how these lyrics came about or how they got published. Instead, we must rely on the subsequent recollections of Colonel John Stuart Skinner in 1849 and those of Roger B. Taney in 1856.[87] The credit for having the lyrics published has been debated between Colonel Skinner and Captain Joseph Hopper Nicholson of the U.S. Volunteers, Baltimore Fencibles.*

In 1972, an authoritative account on this subject was published. It claimed that "on the morning after Key's return…Key took the poem to Judge Joseph Hopper Nicholson of Baltimore."[88] But did he?

Skinner was the U.S. agent for prisoner exchange and led the effort to seek the release of an American doctor captured by the British as they withdrew back to their ships after occupying Washington. Skinner was present with Key during the bombardment of Fort McHenry. They were retained onboard the American flag-of-truce packet vessel* *President*, anchored to the east side of the British fleet lying about two miles below the fort. Upon their

Francis Scott Key observing the bombardment of Fort McHenry. *Percy E. Moran, Library of Congress.*

release, Skinner accompanied Key to the Indian Queen Hotel in Baltimore. Thirty-five years later, in 1849, Skinner wrote:

> [W]*e got back to Baltimore, in the hotel then kept at the corner of Hanover and Market Streets, was but a versified and almost literal transcript of our expressed hopes and apprehensions, through that ever-*

memorable period of anxiety to all but never of despair. Calling on its accomplished author the next morning, he handled [sic] it [the lyrics] to the undersigned [Skinner], who passed it on to the Baltimore Patriot, and through it to immortality.[89]

One might think that Roger B. Taney would have been biased in his memory since he and Key had both married Lloyd family sisters and were former law partners in Frederick, Maryland. In 1856, forty-two years after the event, Taney wrote that Nicholson had printed the handbills:

The judge [Nicholson] had been relieved from duty [at Fort McHenry] and returned to his family only the night before Mr. Key showed him the song. And you may easily imagine the feeling with which, at such a moment, he read it and gave it to the public. In less than an hour after it was placed in the hands of the printer, it [the handbill broadside] was all over town.[90]

George J. Svejda wrote in 1969, "It would seem impossible for Judge [Captain Joseph H.] Nicholson, as Taney relates, to have sent Key's poem to the printer because the former was then engaged with his military duties at Fort McHenry." Svejda points out that Thomas Marsh Forman, in a letter addressed to Nicholson on September 15, stopped by to see Nicholson at 1:00 p.m. that very day and "found the house closed."[91]

Captain Nicholson's militia* artillery company was stationed at Fort McHenry with the regular U.S. garrison. On September 17, when the British fleet weighed anchor off North Point and set sail down the Chesapeake, Nicholson would have been fully engaged in taking care of his company. He had one man killed and two wounded in addition to his normal duties as captain. After the battle, Major Armistead was "in a high state of delirium," causing Nicholson to serve as acting commander. It was Nicholson who wrote a dispatch for an officer to take over command of the fort.[92] On September 18, Nicholson wrote to the secretary of war praising Armistead's conduct, entreating the secretary "not to let him be neglected."[93] With all that was going on at Fort McHenry at this time, it seems unlikely that Nicholson would have returned to Baltimore upon Key's return. Taney's memory appears to be faulty, and thus it seems likely that Skinner, not Nicholson, took Key's lyrics to have them printed.

HMS Minden: A Case of Mistaken Identity

In January 1863, during the height of the Civil War, William Curtis Naps sent a letter to President Abraham Lincoln. It set off a long and confused belief that the HM ship of the line* Minden was the vessel that Francis Scott Key was aboard when he wrote "The Star-Spangled Banner." Below is part of that letter:

> Sir, the frigate* "Minden" of the British Navy was engaged in the Bombardment of Baltimore during the last war with England, and the late F.S. Key, the author of the celebrated National Ode, "The Star-Spangled Banner," was kept under her guns and compelled to witness the attempted destruction of that city, having gone to her with a flag of truce to release a friend. While in this condition, he wrote the music if not the whole of that great & stirring song. The "Minden" was recently broken up at Canton [China in 1859], and a friend new in that country, a Mr. Henry Dwight Williams, has sent to me for your acceptance a cane made from one of the timbers. In presenting it, I congradulate [sic] you on the completion of your great act of emancipation and believe it will bring to the aid of the Government and the cause of freedom & Constitutional liberty, m__ "hearts of oak" than are necessary to crushing out this unholy slaveholding rebellion. I have the honor to be with great respect, Your friend & Servant Wm. Curtis Naps.[94]

Research has confirmed that Minden was not part of the British fleet that attacked Fort McHenry, nor was the ship even in North American waters during the War of 1812. Minden was a seventy-four-gun ship of the line* named after the thirteenth-century German town of Minden. The Minden had been built in 1810 at Bombay, India, in the shipyards of Jamshedji Bomanji Wadia. It ended its career as a hospital ship in Hong Kong and was sold for scrap in 1860. Minden was not known to have ever been in the Chesapeake Bay.

Based on Naps's letter, Colonel John L. Warner read a paper before the Pennsylvania Historical Society in 1867 in which he too stated that Key "was received with courtesy on board the Minden, Admiral Cockburn's flagship...[and] while pacing the deck of the cartel ship* Minden, between midnight and dawn, that Key composed the song." These two instances illustrate examples of misinformation being repeated during the mid- to late nineteenth century—misinformation that writers borrowed for the centennial celebration of the War of 1812.[95]

Cartel packet *President* shown flying an American flag among the British fleet during the bombardment of Fort McHenry. *Courtesy of Maryland Historical Society.*

In the post–Civil War Years, even Key's eldest daughter, Elizabeth Phoebe (Key) Howard (1803–1898), in whose Baltimore Mount Vernon Place home her father died in 1843, continued the story of the *Minden*. She wrote in a letter, "The name of the ship my father went on when he boarded the British fleet was called the Minden."[96]

The *Minden* story was repeated with one major critical change in an 1874 publication by Colonel John Thomas Scharf entitled *The Chronicles of Baltimore: Being A Complete History of "Baltimore Town" and Baltimore City*. In it he wrote, "[Francis Scott Key] having gone on board in the cartel ship *Minden*, in the company of Col. John S. Skinner." The large British ship of the line had now become a small American cartel ship.

The vessel that carried Key and Colonel John Stuart Skinner to their rendezvous with history was the sloop* packet* *President*, one of Benjamin and John Ferguson's Norfolk packets that had been used by Skinner as a cartel ship on earlier diplomatic missions.[97] On September 5, Key and Skinner were sent on a mission to seek the release of a Dr. William Beanes, who had been taken captive in Upper Marlboro for having played a role in arresting British stragglers after the occupation of Washington. The men began their mission at Fells Point (Baltimore), where they boarded the packet* and sailed south to find the British fleet off the mouth of the Potomac River. That they succeeded is confirmed by the logbook of HM frigate* *Surprise*, dated September 8, 1814. The entry reads, "Sent a vessel and the marines to take charge of a sloop with a flag at 7:30 [p.m.] and took her in tow."[98] The term "flag" in this case means a white flag, signifying the sloop was a truce vessel and not a warship.

Adding further to the Francis Scott Key confusion is one of several artifacts known to have been made from *Minden*—a mirror framed by the carved patriotic motif of an eagle. On the back of the motif, an old tag read, "This frame designed by William Speiden and made by a Chinaman in Hong Kong, from the wood of the ship 'Minden,' on board of which was written 'The Star-Spangled Banner.'"[99] Who put the tag on the mirror is unknown, but it was obviously not original to the mirror.

The story does not end here, because Francis Scott Key, John Stuart Skinner and Dr. William Beanes were not alone in observing the bombardment of Fort McHenry. There were nine American crewmen whose names have been all but forgotten: James Gramatt, Thomas Harrison, James Butler, William Marton, Francis Wilkerson, John Porter, Richard Arrol, Nicholas Walker and Jonathan Merar. The British did not release the men until after the bombardment was over and the fleet was withdrawing back down the Patapsco River. During the bombardment, they were apparently anchored to the side of the British fleet. They all saw the Congreve Rocket's* red glare, bursting mortar bombs and cannons firing on Fort McHenry. It gave them a perspective that no other American had during those fateful twenty-five hours—an American perspective from the British fleet. This also means that all the artists' renditions showing Key and Skinner (and sometimes Beanes) watching the bombardment from a British warship are inaccurate because they were in fact onboard a small American cartel ship named *President*.

Surrender of Fort McHenry

On August 28, 1814, former U.S. Congressman Captain Joseph Hopper Nicholson (1770–1817), commander of a company of U.S. Volunteers at Fort McHenry, wrote a letter to his former colleague, Secretary of the Navy William Jones. The letter was in response to having learned that his political enemy, Major General Samuel Smith, had been given command of Baltimore's defense. In the letter, Nicholson expressed not only his displeasure with this appointment but also pointed out the possible regrettable consequences of putting Smith in command. He wrote that Smith would "surrender [Baltimore] without a struggle" and that what was needed was "a commander who has nerve and judgment and if [British] General Ross had marched to this place [Baltimore] instead of the Patuxent he would have been master of our city with less trouble than he had at Washington."[100] Nicholson continued his protest to Secretary of State James Monroe, who, following the resignation of Secretary of War John Armstrong on August 29, 1814, assumed the duties of secretary of war as well. Nicholson wrote:

I pressed General Smith's total incapacity upon Gen'l Armstrong last summer. It becomes a matter of importance that the Government should look into this thing. Now that Gen'l Armstrong is out of the administration, there is not a man left in it that Smith is not hostile to. If an attack is made, he will have a theme for self applause which he will not fail to use. His camp is filled with confusion and is more dangerous to our citizens than the enemy. The troops are not organized; they will afford no protection and had better be sent home than kept here as they are now. Gen'l Smith will boast hereafter that he sustained credit (the pecuniary credit) of the government [for saving Baltimore].[101]

Despite Nicholson's letters and pleas, the military and city leaders selected his rival Smith to command the defense of the city. Both Smith and Nicholson had been political enemies since 1809, when Nicholson implied that Smith's firm, Smith and Buchanan, had been involved in unscrupulous business trade with Europe. To complicate matters, Smith's brother Robert, also a partner in the firm, was at the same time serving as U.S. secretary of the navy.[102]

Nicholson's accusation resurfaced after the Battle for Baltimore when Smith informed Major George Armistead, commander of Fort McHenry, that vicious rumors were again being circulated stating that Smith had ordered Armistead to surrender Fort McHenry. To end these damaging rumors, Smith wrote Armistead on November 6, 1815, stating that, "The story was so very silly that I paid no attention to it."[103] Armistead supported Smith's defense when he replied in writing that the rumors were nonsense. Armistead wrote, "I cannot conceive how such calumny [to blacken another's reputation] could gain belief in the mind of any person, certainly no such advice was ever given or insinuated by you or me."[104]

The myth that Major General Smith, considered a hero for his defense of Baltimore, would surrender Fort McHenry is hard for anyone to believe today and apparently was so in 1814 and early 1815. The publishing of the letter by Major Armistead seems to have done its job, as nothing more was said or published about the rumor.

Captain McPherson and His Flag

Since 1878, stories have been told that a Captain William McPherson (1795–1878) "had in his possession ever since the war [of 1812] an immense flag, which he highly prized, the one that floated over Fort McHenry on that memorable occasion and at his request was buried with him."[105] The story first appeared in McPherson's obituary in 1878. At the time, the Star-Spangled Banner was owned by Major George Armistead's grandson, Eben Appleton Armistead, a prominent banker in New York City. But Captain McPherson's widow, Hannah, "claimed the famous flag" was not in the possession of Mr. Appleton but "is wrapped around the body of her husband and buried with him in [Baltimore's] Green Mount Cemetery."[106]

The story was told in a variety of newspaper columns over the next ninety-five years until the last mention in 1973.[107] Among the variations of the story is that when McPherson died, "the flag was placed on the top of Captain McPherson's coffin after it had been lowered into the grave" and that a British mortar shell, recovered from Fort McHenry after the bombardment,* was also buried with him at his request.[108] Another version suggests, "wrapped around his casket were the remains of the original Star-Spangled Banner that floated from his home in South Baltimore."[109] When he died, McPherson's wife stated that the flag had been reduced to a size of forty by eighteen feet due to souvenirs having been given away.[110]

Mrs. McPherson stated that on national holidays, her husband displayed the flag in front of his residence and that "his chief delight on such occasions was while occupying a comfortable seat, smoking his pipe, to gaze at the 'immortal banner' and recite war reminiscences."[111] Mrs. McPherson also claimed that her husband had served in the U.S. Army and was at Fort McHenry during the bombardment and had been presented with the flag afterward.

This is a fascinating story, but one not supported by the facts. There is no record of any McPherson at Fort McHenry during the bombardment. Only his obituary makes the claim that he "was a captain in the regular army in the war of 1812–14 and took part in the defense of Fort McHenry." If he were born in 1795, he would have been nineteen years old at the time of the bombardment. It seems unlikely that a nineteen-year-old would have been given such an important memento after the bombardment. However, there may be a clue as to how this tale came about.

Although little is known about McPherson, there was a man by that name who was the proprietor of the Mount Clare Hotel in June 1842. He received thanks from various militia* companies who had participated in the Grand Encampment of 1842, a military rendezvous held on the historic grounds of Mount Clare. Was the flag he cherished one that had been given him at the Grand Encampment rather than from the War of 1812?[112] On January 13, 1902, Hannah M. McPherson died and was buried in Green Mount Cemetery with a piece of a flag, about one foot square, placed in her coffin.[113]

A Baltimore newspaper article dated November 8, 1973, stated that a seven-inch remnant of a flag, framed and signed by an unnamed ancestor in 1873, was presented to the descendants of Captain William McPherson. The article states, "The story I was told by my dad is that this guy McPherson supposedly reached up from his horse, grabbed a corner of the flag, and cut it off with his saber. I don't know if it is true. But it's not hard to imagine that he was simply out to get himself a souvenir of the battle."[114] The article goes on to claim that the flag remnant was displayed at the 1915 Panama-Pacific International Exposition in San Francisco. At some point, the flag remnant was supposedly authenticated by the Smithsonian Institution.

The replica of the Star-Spangled Banner that flies from the one-hundred-foot flagstaff at Fort McHenry has the same dimensions as the original—thirty by forty-two feet. On a calm day, the lowest hanging end of the Star-Spangled Banner would have been at least fifty feet above McPherson, even if he were on horseback. While it is possible that Captain McPherson was buried with a cut-off souvenir scrap of the Star-Spangled Banner or, more likely, a different American flag, he certainly was not buried with the Star-Spangled Banner flag, as it resides today at the Smithsonian Institution.

Since the early nineteenth century, it was not uncommon to see a flag of such large dimensions. A possible clue to this story is that there was indeed another flag at Fort McHenry during the 1814 bombardment. This flag, known as a storm flag, measured seventeen by twenty-five feet. Its whereabouts are unknown, but having no special attachment or interest at the time, it may have been properly disposed of as any flag would have been. Could the flag that the McPhersons talked about have been the storm flag? Or could it have been a flag given to him from the Grand Encampment of 1842? The tale told in the obituary appears to be a confusion of McPherson's flag with the Star-Spangled Banner, embellished over time to make a good story by a family who loved and cherished their relative. To this day, older visitors to Fort McHenry still ask about the truth behind the story of Captain William McPherson and his flag.

Fishing for Cannon

In 1873, a dredging machine working in Baltimore Harbor brought up five cannons off Jackson's Wharf in Fells Point. A newspaper reported, "From the thick crust of rust which has formed upon them and eaten the metal away, as well, their antique fashion, it is evident that they are very old and were probably used in the war between the United States and England in 1812–14." The article adds, "A legend exists in the neighborhood that in the War of 1812, a battery of six guns stood in the vicinity of Jackson's Wharf, and it is supposed that the guns brought up originally belonged to that battery."[115]

There were, in fact, several gun batteries* in addition to Fort McHenry that helped to defend Baltimore during the War of 1812, but none were located at Fells Point. This legend apparently stems from a six-gun battery named Fort Babcock, built to defend the west flank of Fort McHenry. But the guns at Fort Babcock are eighteen-pounder* guns, far too large and heavy to have been brought up by a harbor dredge "scoop." This is an example of someone jumping to a conclusion to explain how the cannons appeared off Jackson's Wharf. More likely, the cannons were used as bollards* to help fasten ship lines to the wharf. Over time and decay, the bollards fell into the harbor. The practice of using cannons for bollards is well known. While these guns may date from the War of 1812, they are too small to have been from a fort and more likely came off Baltimore privateers. Throughout Baltimore, such cannons were used to memorialize War of 1812 centennial monuments around the city and can be found at Patterson Park, Riverside Park, the Fort Babcock site and Canton Wharf. It is very possible that the five cannons dredged up in 1873 are among those in these settings today.

Cannons mounted at Patterson Park may be dredged cannons from Baltimore Harbor. *Ralph Eshelman photograph.*

BALTIMORE COUNTY

British Soldiers and the Todd House Graveyard

The Bernard Todd House, located on North Point Road near where the British landed on September 12, 1814, to march on Baltimore, served as a horse courier station to report British ship movements during the war. In retaliation for these military activities, the British burned the house and the outbuildings, forcing the family to live in a granary for two years while the present house was built.

In 1907, the *Baltimore Sun* reported that the Todd House "was burned to the ground by the British." It continued:

Todd graveyard with Todd House in the background. The house was built on the foundation of the original house, which was burned by the British in 1814. *Ralph Eshelman photograph.*

The family had some servants [who] *had fled to Mrs. Thomas B. Todd's country residence, in the neighborhood of Gatche's Meeting House* [location unknown]. *When they returned, they found the lands devastated, the sheep and cattle had been driven in the well-stored granary and afterward killed. A body was exhumed in the old family burying ground, adjoining the house, which the men* [British] *had dug up with their bayonets, thinking there was silver buried within. After replacing the coffin, one of the men remarked: "It was only an old lady peacefully asleep."*[116]

When private property losses could be proven to be the result of military use during war, the U.S. government sometimes compensated the owner. In 1853, Bernard Todd's heirs received $4,315, the appraised value of the burned property, because in this case, the house had been used as a military courier station. However, the story of British troops using bayonets to dig up a grave to find buried silver, published ninety-three years after the event, is not supported by contemporary documents.

One of the Todd family members married a sister of Major Jonas Green of the 6th Maryland Cavalry from Baltimore County. The home of Major Green stood on the south side of Bear Creek. It was supposedly saved from burning by the British because of the pleadings and shrewdness of an old man left in charge after the family had taken refuge at a summer residence. The unidentified man told the British that the house was a home for orphans.

Eleanor Escapes the Advances of a British Officer

Thomas Shaw (1745–1829) owned a circa 1800 farmhouse on the south side of North Point Road. It was along this road that more than four thousand British troops marched from North Point toward Baltimore on the morning of September 12, 1814. The Shaws were probably aware of a possible British attack on Baltimore since rumors were circulating all around. Only a few miles to the south, at North Point, was a lookout post and nearby courier station (Todd House) to alert Baltimore of enemy movements on the Patapsco River. Still, Mr. Shaw and his family could not have expected what would happen later that morning.

According to legend, Major General Robert Ross, commander of the British land forces, stopped at the Shaw house to rest. Ross and his staff took possession of the first floor, pressing the occupants upstairs. A British lieutenant supposedly met Shaw's daughter Eleanor on the staircase and attempted to kiss her. Eleanor resisted these advances and fled out of the house by jumping from the second-floor window. General Ross immediately ordered the officer arrested and taken back to the ship to await disciplinary action. The legend continues that Eleanor possessed a nightcap that Ross had left behind that morning.

This story was first revealed by the Reverend Lewis Beeman Browne, rector of the Protestant Episcopal Church at Sparrow's Point, in a 1907 article titled "Battle of North Point in Legend and Tradition" and later retold in a lecture given by General R. Williams at the Maryland Historical Society in 1914.[117]

Would a panicked young lady actually jump out of a second-story window? It seems more likely that she would have run up the stairs to the safety of her parents and remained with them. By jumping outside, she would have placed herself among strange and possibly hated British troops. The story is retold in a children's book published in 1966 wherein the officer who

When a British officer attempts to kiss Eleanor, she jumps to escape her pursuer. © *Gerry Embleton illustration.*

tried to kiss Eleanor is identified as Lieutenant McGregor. When Eleanor jumps from the second-story window, there is an added twist, as she lands in a rain barrel full of feathers.[118] If General Ross carried a nightcap with him during his planned assault on Baltimore, no such nightcap is known to exist today. This legend seems doubtful, but the Dundalk Patapsco Neck Historical Society has a window frame said to be the very window frame through which Eleanor escaped her pursuer.

The Shaw family resided at the Thomas Shaw house until 1885, when it was purchased by the Foulke family. A small family cemetery is located on the road leading to the house site.[119] In 1914, the farm was owned by Elmer Stansbury before being acquired by the Bethlehem Steel Corporation for expansion of its facilities. The house was torn down in 1976, leaving only the brick foundation that remains today. The Maryland Department of Natural Resources administers the site as part of the North Point State Park.

Sup in Baltimore or in Hell

One of the more legendary quotations associated with the War of 1812 on the Chesapeake is the reputed statement by British Major General Robert Ross, who is said to have proclaimed as he marched toward Baltimore that he did "not care if it rains militia" and "I shall sup in Baltimore to-night, or in hell." The origin of these statements is unclear, and they may have come from different sources. The earliest known quote of "rains militia" appeared in Hezekiah Niles's weekly magazine on September 24, 1814, twelve days after the event, in which he stated, "Major general Ross, who did 'not care if it rained militia,' the incendiary of the capitol, paid the forfeit of that act by his death."[120]

Another version of this quote is found in the oration of H. Clay Dallam, who stated in 1878, "The prisoners [American dragoons*] were taken before General Ross, to whom they gave an exaggerated account of the strength of the American forces. 'But they are mainly militia I presume,' observed General Ross. They replied in the affirmative, and General Ross said that he would take Baltimore 'if it rains militia.'"[121]

The earliest quote of "I shall sup in Baltimore" appears to have come from John Henry Willis Hawkins (1797–1858), a seventeen-year-old private in Captain James Haslett's company, 2nd Maryland Regiment. Hawkins worked as an apprentice hatter in Baltimore, and his brother-in-law, Dr. Samuel B. Martin, served as a surgeon in Major William Pinckney's 1st Maryland Rifle Battalion, in which Hawkins had volunteered. Hawkins's son, Reverend William George, who published a biography of his father in 1859, wrote the following account:

> *Dr. Martin, a few days after the battle, rode down to North Point, to the residence of Mr. Gorsuch, at whose house General Ross and his fellow officers had breakfasted on the morning of the twelfth and learned from him the following facts. On their departure for the field of battle, Mr. Gorsuch asked the General if he should prepare supper for them upon their return. "No," said he; "I shall sup in Baltimore to-night, or in hell!"*[122]

The 1859 Hawkins narrative is apparently also the origin of the story that early in the day on September 12, word had passed along the American lines, "Remember boys, General Ross rides a white horse today!" Ross actually rode a black horse.

Major General Robert Ross. *Portrait owned by Stephen Campbell. Courtesy of Christopher George.*

It is hoped that other early references to these quotes can be found, but with the information presently at hand, it appears that the "rains militia" quote occurred not more than ten days after the event and may actually be true, although possibly attributed to the wrong officer (see below). The "sup in Baltimore" quote appeared forty-five years after the event and is probably not true. Since 1859, these combined quotes have been used repeatedly by numerous authors.[123] Such bombastic remarks would not have been expected from the mild-mannered General Ross and are more in the style of Rear Admiral George Cockburn.[124]

General Ross's Last Breath

The most significant British officer killed in the Chesapeake during the War of 1812 was Major General Robert Ross, commander of the British land forces during the Battle for Baltimore. There have always been questions as to the exact location where General Ross was shot and where he died (see also "Who Killed General Ross?"). A historic roadside marker located approximately at the 4630 block of North Point Boulevard supposedly marks the location of his death, about 1.5 miles southeast of where he was wounded. The marker, however, has been moved from its original location at least three times. The first and presumably most accurate location was approximately fifty feet east of North Point Boulevard, near the north end of the present-day DAP Inc. fence line.[125]

The only marker near the location where Ross presumably was shot is a memorial to twenty-four-year-old Maryland militiaman Aquila Randall, who fell during the same skirmish preceding the Battle of North Point (the land component of the Battle for Baltimore—the bombardment* of Fort McHenry was the naval component). The Aquila monument was also moved, but only about one hundred feet north of its original location. Thus, the only monument at the skirmish site memorializes Private Aquila Randall—not Major General Robert Ross.

After General Ross had been shot, he was placed "on a stretcher made of two fence rails from the spot where he was [mortally] wounded to Poplar Heights, about a mile and a half to the rear; but when the cart arrived, he was already dead. The bearers laid their burden under a poplar tree by the wayside opposite Gorsuch's farm."[126] The poplar tree location is believed to have originated in an article published in 1844:

> [T]he large wild poplar tree, under which the British General Ross...drew his last breath. The old tree, after weathering thirty winters...has fallen under the stroke of the woodsman's ax. It was situated on the land of Mr. Vincent Green. We doubt whether there is to be found in the country a tree under which "confusion to the enemies of liberty" has been quaffed in full bumpers more frequently than under "Ross' Tree," as it has always been familiarly called.[127]

The poplar tree story was retold by Reverend Lewis B. Browne in 1907. Browne stated that the tree stood on a high roadside earthen embankment near the intersection of present-day Wise Avenue and North Point Road.

1850s image of the Aquila Randall Monument, near where Major General Robert Ross was mortally wounded. Taken from *Lossing's Pictorial Field-Book of the War of 1812*.

The tree's long branches hung over the road, on which the British army had marched under them. This location is about a half mile north of where the historic marker for General Ross's death is located. It appears that Reverend Browne's 1907 account of the location of the poplar tree is inaccurate since it is too far north of the presumed General Ross death site.

The poplar tree under which Ross was mortally wounded died in 1844. Vincent Green, the landowner, ordered his overseer to cut the tree down to keep it from being a hazard to passersby. One 1844 newspaper stated, "Such was the veneration in which it was held that many individuals secured pieces as relics."[128]

Regardless of the exact location of the tree, it is known that a cart was procured from a nearby farm, and the body of General Ross was conveyed to a landing and then to the British fleet. Ross's remains were taken onboard HM ship of the line* *Royal Oak* at 9:00 p.m.[129] Major General Robert Ross was buried at Halifax, Nova Scotia, far from his home in Ireland (see also "A Bag of Coins and Horse, Cart and Blankets").

Who Killed General Ross?

Major General Robert Ross was the commander of the British land forces who attempted to take Baltimore on September 12, 1814. The popular and well-respected forty-eight-year-old general had been mortally wounded in a skirmish prior to the Battle of North Point (the land component of the Battle for Baltimore), and his troops were shocked and in mourning. The unexpected and the unthinkable had happened. We will never know how the outcome of the Battle for Baltimore might have changed if Ross had not been killed, but we do know that while the British won the Battle of North Point, they lost the Battle for Baltimore. Who killed Ross—and what were the circumstances?

Since the Battle of North Point nearly two hundred years ago, the circumstances surrounding the death of General Ross (1766–1814) have captivated Baltimoreans. For residents who live near the site, the story is as true as if they and prior generations had witnessed it. Here is the popular story. Both the Americans and the British sent advance parties forward. About noon, they encountered one another, and shots were fired. General Ross was riding forward to investigate when he fell from his horse after being hit. Two youths, Privates Daniel Wells and Henry G. McComas of Captain Edward Aisquith's Sharpshooters, firing simultaneously, had found their mark, one of them felling Ross from his horse with a single rifle ball. The British returned fire, killing nineteen-year-old Wells and eighteen-year-old McComas.

A May 21, 1813 article in the *Washington Daily National Intelligencer*, written by a British officer more than a year before the skirmish, stated, "Their [American] muskets, which are of large caliber, carry fifteen large buck shot besides a ball and make tremendous havoc [upon human flesh]."[130] A narrative by a British officer on October 28, 1814, a month after the skirmish, stated, "General Ross was killed by a shot from a boy behind a tree."[131]

On November 4, 1815, a year after the event, an article signed "A Sharpshooter" appeared in a Baltimore newspaper:

> *I perceived by the last London Papers, that the officers, non-commissioned officers and privates, of the 20th regt. British Foot, have erected a Monument to the memory of Gen. Ross, one Lieut. Col. of that regt. In the Parish Church of Ross Trevor [Rostrevor], the place of the General's birth; by an inscription upon which it appears, that, Major Gen. Ross was killed*

87

1819 romanticized print depicting Major General Ross falling into the arms of another officer while a Congreve Rocket passes overhead. *Courtesy of Library of Congress.*

by a Rifle Ball, which must silence the pretension, of the [American] *Infantry Companies employed on the advance and yield the honor to the two Gallant Riflemen (Sharpshooters) whose lives paid for the forfeit of their devotion and gallantry.*[132]

The monument to General Ross referred to in the article is located in Kilbroney Parish Church in Rostrevor, Northern Ireland. However, the inscription does not mention "a rifle ball." It simply states that Ross "fell on the 12th of September 1814." One could easily jump to the conclusion that the sharpshooter's claim is false. However, the original suggested text for the monument does include the words "wounded by a rifle ball in the approaches of Baltimore on the 12th of September, 1814." That inscription was published in the *Norfolk American Beacon* (and probably other newspapers as well) on September 31, 1815, over a month before the sharpshooter's letter. The final inscription on the monument was shortened, leaving out the reference "rifle ball."[133]

Two days later, "The Sharpshooter" was debated by a reader who signed his name "One of the Infantry." The unidentified individual was a member of Captain Benjamin C. Howard's First Mechanical Volunteers. In the article, he poses the following:

It is not to be supposed that the ball itself was ever discovered—have never heard that his body was dissected, and hence it is probable that the size of the wound was the only method of determining the nature of the ball. But everyone knows that the British musket bullets are much larger than ours, and when we add to this the reflection that all gun shot wounds close in some degree from the elasticity of flesh immediately after the ball has passed thro', it accounts easily for the opinion that the wound was given from a rifle…whilst in the infantry companies many can now be found who aimed and fired at the only officer who was visible on horseback, and who therefore in all probability, must have been General Ross.[134]

Thus, by early 1815, the testy disagreement had begun between the Sharpshooters and the First Mechanical Volunteers as to who deserves the credit for having shot General Ross. On the occasion of the laying of the cornerstone of the North Point Monument at Battle Acre in 1839, Captain Howard made the following remarks:

A story obtained partial currency at the time, and perhaps may yet be repeated, that he [Ross] *was slain by some person who had climbed a tree and was thus enabled to overlook the ground. Nothing can be more absurd or ridiculous than this idle tale. There was neither time nor motive for anyone to adopt such a device. The British general was slain in fair and open combat by those whose persons were as much exposed as his own, and it is hoped that the preposterous and derogatory story will never again be mentioned.*[135]

In 1872, a twenty-one-foot-tall obelisk was constructed for the two boy heroes. Called the Wells and McComas Monument, it still stands today in Ashland Square, Baltimore. On the occasion of their reinterment in this new location, a play was written in their honor entitled *The Boy Martyrs of Sept. 12, 1814: A Local Historical Drama in Three Acts.* Interestingly, the monument does not claim Wells or McComas as having fired the shot (or shots) that killed General Ross. Despite this, one author goes so far as to claim the killing of General Ross by these two boys "demoralized the invading forces and as a result they retreated to their ships and left the country." He continues by stating that if this incident happened today, Wells and McComas would be candidates for the Medal of Honor.[136]

There is an interesting sidebar to the Daniel Wells story. A Baltimore newspaper published an article exactly one year prior to the skirmish at North Point in which it detailed the arrest of Daniel Wells—probably the same Daniel Wells who died in 1814—for failing to muster with his militia unit. Taken before a judge, Daniel was "remanded to his officer, and conducted to camp."[137]

A second monument is dedicated to another militiaman who died in the same skirmish. This monument commemorates twenty-four-year-old Aquila Randall, who some claim killed General Ross. This small marble monument, erected in 1817, was one of the first monuments erected on an American battlefield. It is located near the site of the skirmish but like the Wells and McComas Monument, it does not claim that the person memorialized had killed Ross.

We will probably never know who actually killed General Ross. Other stories claim Ross was killed by friendly fire—still another that Ross was hit by canister* shot.[138] As with many legends, it is easy to assume that because a monument was built for someone who died in action he must have been the person who fired the mortal shot that killed General Ross. While it is possible, there is no documentary evidence to resolve this open question. For many of the youth of Baltimore County, however, there is no doubt as to who killed the general, because Wells and McComas were given the credit in a 1966 children's book about the war. The title page states, "For

Boys and Girls Intermediate Grades—Junior High School."[139] Indeed, as the epigraph of this book (not the children's book) proclaims, "When the legend becomes fact, print the legend."

A Bag of Coins and Horse, Cart and Blankets

After Major General Robert Ross was mortally wounded in a skirmish prior to the Battle of North Point (see also "General Ross's Last Breath"), a horse, cart and blankets were procured to take the general's body back to the British fleet. Where did this horse and cart come from? There are at least three different versions. The earliest known origin of the horse-and-cart story appeared in the 1907 Baltimore and Ohio Railroad publication *Book of the Royal Blue*.[140] In it, Reverend Lewis Beeman Browne wrote that the British went to the estate of Abraham Stansbury (1746/47–1811), a one-storied house known as Twin Oaks that faced Back River. There were two roads that led to the farm, one from North Point Road and one from Poplar Heights, near where General Ross died. British soldiers reportedly committed depredations at the house such as slashing feather beds. One chap was said to have taken a chest, but upon finding it locked, he threatened to open it by force. The lady of the household, presumably Mrs. Elizabeth Stansbury (c. 1775–c. 1822), informed the soldier that it contained a small bag of gunpowder and shot and offered to open the chest with her key if she could keep the bag, allowing the thief to keep whatever else he wanted in the chest. To this the soldier agreed, allowing Mrs. Stansbury to take not a bag of shot but a bag of coins.

After an interval of several hours, to the surprise of the Stansburys, the British returned just prior to the beginning of the Battle of North Point and asked for the loan of a horse and cart as well as some blankets. Afterward, the cart and horse were returned, the family learning that they had been used to carry the body of Major General Ross back to the British fleet. But the story does not end here. The Dundalk Patapsco Neck Historical Society claims that the horse, cart and blankets came from the Trotten farmhouse, located on Bear Creek near Pennwood Road at the present-day location of the Bethlehem Steel Corporation plant.[141] The claim is very similar to the Stansbury account but contains some interesting twists. After partaking of some wine, pickles and preserves, one British soldier supposedly chalked on the front door, "We have found very good cheer with Mrs. Trotten and hope she be at home when we return." A few hours later, soldiers did return, but this time they demanded a horse, cart and some blankets. To Sarah Trotten's surprise, the British returned the items and she learned that they had been used to convey General Ross's body to the fleet.

Finally, there is a third version from a newspaper account written in 1911 that states that a carriage and horses were obtained from the George Stansbury house that later became known as the old Battleground House, located near the spot where General Ross was wounded.[142] And just to make things even more interesting, the Shaw house was owned by Elmer Stansbury. Many Stansburys owned houses in this area over the years.

These versions are all similar, but they do have some particular differences. The Trotten farmhouse and Twin Oaks homes are situated off the known route used by the British in their march to Baltimore. Stansbury's Twin Oaks is located on Back River on the northeast side of the Patapsco Peninsula, whereas Trotten's farmhouse is located on Bear Creek on the southwest side of the peninsula. Battleground House is probably the same as Dr. Houck's Pavilion (Battleground Hotel), which is distinct from Monument Hotel (it gets complicated). Battleground House is along the known British route. There is evidence that the British used Bear Creek and possibly Colgate Creek to evacuate wounded, resupply the land troops and pass communications. Both creeks are off the Patapsco River on the southwest side of the peninsula, where the fleet was located. It seems reasonable that Ross's body would have been conveyed to the fleet in the easiest way possible, which would have been a water route. We may never know for sure from which house the British took a horse, cart and blankets. Battleground House is located closest to where Ross was shot, but why is this connection not mentioned before 1911? It's also interesting that this account for the first time states a "carriage" instead of cart and "horses" instead of horse. The Battleground House and Trotten farmhouse seem to be the most reasonable locations for this incident to have occurred. Could Reverend Browne have confused the houses? Or was the confusion already present when he heard the story and repeated it ninety-three years after the event? We know that other accounts Browne repeated in his 1907 publication are inaccurate (see "General Ross's Last Breath").

All three houses are unfortunately gone. The cause of the demise of Twin Oaks is unknown. Battleground House was set on fire by an arsonist in 1911. The Trotten farmhouse was later used as the clubhouse for the Sparrows Point Country Club before burning down in 1954.

Saved by a Silver Pencil Holder

Family tradition claims that Nathaniel Williams (1772–1859) was saved by the deflection of a musket ball by "a silver lead pencil" holder he carried in his vest pocket during the Battle of North Point. Could such a story be true?

According to the story, Nathaniel returned to Baltimore from Annapolis, where he was serving in the senate of the Maryland General Assembly, joining his colleagues in the defense of Baltimore. His patriotism was magnified, as politicians were exempt from the call to arms. After she bade her husband farewell, Caroline Barney Williams (1788–1825) became stricken with fear for his safety, closed the door and "dropped limp in a swoon."[143]

Caroline's fears proved true. During the battle, her beloved Nathaniel was wounded by British musket fire. He was found lying upon the battlefield, apparently dead, conscious but unable to speak. Two British soldiers approached him, and one of them commented, "He is good as dead." He took Williams's canteen, which was filled with brandy, and left him to die. However, the musket ball that had hit him had been deflected by "a silver lead pencil" holder he carried in his vest pocket.

At first glance, this story appears to be another family tradition, complete with a wife "swooning" when her husband left for war. But there is more. Williams had served as a private in Lieutenant Commander John Reese's company of the 5th Maryland Regiment at the Battle of North Point. In a petition for a pension, Dr. William Owens, surgeon of the 5th Regiment, stated that Williams had "received a bullet wound, deep seated in his hip near the joint" and in his opinion "was in two-thirds degree, disabled from obtaining his subsistence by manual labor." In the aftermath of the Battle of North Point, Adjutant John Barney and Dr. Williams found Nathaniel "in a log cabin near the place of action, severely and dangerously wounded; that he was disabled from rising, not having had for forty-eight hours any surgical aid; that he was placed on a bed, put into a horse cart" and returned home to his wife.[144]

Did the silver pencil holder save Nathaniel's life? Since he was wounded in the hip and was said to have carried his silver pencil holder in his vest pocket, the implication is that the holder deflected a bullet from his chest to his hip. According to legend, the silver pencil holder remains with the family as a memento of Nathaniel Williams's close encounter with death. Perhaps the Williams family still possesses this memento and will contact the authors to help substantiate the story of the silver pencil holder.[145]

How Did Bread and Cheese Creek Get Its Name?

Just to the north of the North Point State Battlefield, where on September 12, 1814, the Baltimore 5th Regiment clashed with the British land forces marching on Baltimore, lies a small creek with an unusual name. How did Bread and Cheese Creek get its name? One version is that the Maryland militia* passed the night prior to the battle eating bread and cheese and partaking of water from a spring at the headwaters of the creek. The earliest published origin of this story is taken from the 1907 Baltimore and Ohio Railroad publication *Book of the Royal Blue*.[146] However, another more likely explanation is that a team of surveyors mapping the area around the creek gave it this name because they had bread and cheese for lunch at the spring. What is known is that the name Bread and Cheese Creek dates to colonial times and therefore was not so named during the Battle of North Point in 1814.[147]

Bread and Cheese Creek, 1973. *Courtesy of Dundalk Patapsco Neck Historical Society.*

CALVERT COUNTY

The Catapult and Abington Manor

One of the more obscure, humorous and yet incredible 1812 stories involves Abington Manor and a militia* attack on a British squadron in which a pine tree was used as a catapult. The story begins on August 22, 1814, along the shore of the Patuxent River, when Rear Admiral George Cockburn ordered the burning of a plantation house known as Abington Manor, now called Woodlawn. A heavy downpour, along with the efforts of the plantation slaves, managed to save most of the house although one wing and the kitchen were completely burned.

The Americans got revenge on the British when the militia sank two ships by setting them on fire by using "a catapult from standing pine saplings, they rained flaming bales of wool, soaked with tar." As the British sailors tried to extinguish the flames, "Marylanders picked them off one-by-one with their squirrel guns." Unable to save the ships, the British scuttled them, "hoping to block the channel."[148]

The engagement "was at a sharp, narrow bend in the river, about a mile and a half upstream from where the bridge [Maryland Route 4] crosses the Pax [Patuxent]. A cousin sawed off the top of the mast of one of them in the 20's and had walking sticks made from it. One anchor was salvaged and forged into a rod, capped by two S shaped irons. This was used to brace the present house, since [a] small crack appeared which was caused by the fire."[149]

Abington Manor supposedly has a "secret panel at the side of one of the living room windows. It is said that the early presidents from Wash. [Washington] to Lincoln were honored guests…and that George Washington was much interested in one of the beautiful Miss Sparrows [who lived at the manor at that time], over whom he reportedly almost fought a duel." A drop-leaf table of black mahogany "said to have been made on the Mayflower on its maiden voyage" was supposedly once part of the furnishings of the manor.[150]

The details of the house, its furnishings and honorary visitors appear to be pure fabrication. The house is believed to date from about 1800, so it is unlikely that the early presidents would have been honored guests—and certainly not George Washington, who died in 1799.

The details of the British raid have a ring of truth but appear to be a melding of two different incidents. The British did ascend the Patuxent on August 22, and the Americans did scuttle their flotilla that day above where the Route 4 bridge crosses the river, but no British ships are known to have been scuttled. Farther downriver at Hollands Cliffs, the militia assembled along the bluffs to ambush a British raiding party as it descended the river after having plundered Lower Marlboro. Runaway slaves warned the British of the American presence, and Royal Marines were landed to flank them. No Americans were found, but a few shots were fired from the wooded heights as the British passed the bluffs. This event took place on June 17, 1814, two months before the above engagement. There is no mention in any contemporary documents of the use of a catapult. Could the heavy rain that is said to have helped put out the flames of Abington Manor be taken from the story of the storm that struck Washington on August 25? (For information about that story, see "Did the Great Storm Put Out the Flames of Washington?") This is an interesting story that must be considered a myth.

CHARLES COUNTY

Mrs. McPherson and Her Pet Monkey

The story of Mrs. McPherson and her pet monkey dates from 1899, when Sister Mary Xavier published a booklet of tales told by her grandmother.[151] In it, "grandma" stated that the British had visited Bryantown during their march from Benedict to Washington in August 1814. Here the British encountered a "very plucky" patriotic woman named McPherson. She had known the ravages of the American Revolution and did not have good feeling in her heart for "Redcoats."

As the British ascended the hill toward her house, she went out to meet them. Mrs. McPherson asked what business they had, and Major General Robert Ross replied, "We are only reconnoitring [sic], madam. Have you any sons?" Mrs. McPherson replied, "Yes, I have one, and he is at the cannon's mouth, ready to put a ball through you or some of your comardes [*sic*]. You have no business on our land; we have never interfered with you and you should have stayed at home, sir." The general smiled and inquired whether she could give them something to eat. She replied, "Yes, I will give you in God's name all I have in my cupboard" and then invited the soldiers inside her house. When they saw a rifle by the door, the general inquired whose it was. Mrs. McPherson replied, "It was my husband's, sir, and he used it well on your people years ago. It was on his shoulder when he saw your Cornwallis give up to Washington at Yorktown." The general then asked if he could have it. She replied, "You'll take my life first, sir. I'll defend it to my last breath, and whoever dares to touch it will feel the weight of my arm." Mrs. McPherson then took a poker from the fireplace and stationed herself next to the rifle by the door. General Ross said, "You are very plucky," upon which she replied, "Yes, and all my people are of the same stamp, and I can tell you, sir, that many of you who have come in to fight us will never go out: your old carcasses will be left on plucky soil."

Mrs. McPherson had a pet monkey named Jacko. When Jacko saw the "Redcoats," he ran to the "tip-top of a large old oak in the front yard and no persuasion or coaxing could get him down." One of the officers said, "I'll bring him down" and fired his gun at the monkey, who fell dead on the ground. Mrs. McPherson "flew to her dear monkey, took it in her arms and turning to the officer, said: 'You scoundrel of a vandal; that shows what you are; what harm did this poor creature do to any of you, you vile rascals. Be gone off my plantation. I'm not afraid of any of your kind, and God grant that you, sir, who killed my poor monkey may soon fall as dead as he is now. Go off, every one of you.'" Ashamed of their brutality, the soldiers hurried off, no doubt not forgetting Mrs. McPherson.

This is a wonderful tale but has no contemporary documentation to support it. The believed route of the British troops to Washington is not through Bryantown but farther to the east. It is possible that some flanking or reconnoitering squads could have made it to Bryantown, but certainly not General Ross. When a dialogue like this is printed, it is almost certain that the writer made up words to reflect the story as he or she remembered it. This fascinating tale cannot yet be documented.

GARRETT COUNTY

Political Fracas at Selbysport

Politics between the anti-war Federalists and pro-war Democratic-Republicans were fierce. We tend to think of western Maryland as exempt from the actions of the War of 1812, which were more focused on the tidewater region of the Chesapeake Bay, but militiamen* were recruited from all around the state, including Selbysport, located in far western Garrett County. Legendary hunter Meshack (also Meshach) Browning (1781–1859), commissioned a captain (sergeant according to some accounts) in the 50th Regiment, Maryland militia, mustered his men at "Selby's Port," then a flourishing river port at the head of navigation on the Youghiogheny River.

Because Browning was an anti-war Federalist, members of the Democratic-Republican Party resented him and instigated a political fracas near a bridge over the Youghiogheny. Forty-seven years after the affair, Browning wrote of his experience:

Trace of the Old Morgantown Road over the Youghiogheny River just west of Selbysport, near where a political fracas occurred in 1812. *Ralph Eshelman photograph.*

These [Democratic-Republicans] *formed two lines on both sides of a [mill] tail-race…about twenty on each side, determined to attack and beat me as I should pass the bridge. Many passes were made at me, but the cowards would run as soon as they struck. Let me turn my face which way I would, it met somebody's fist. Let them beat away; but once in a while, I would get a chance at one who would be exposed and give him a good send. This happened about the middle of November* [1812], *and I was not able to carry firewood till the first of May following.*[152]

Tradition holds that Browning won the fracas but was so badly injured that it ended his military career. Near Selbysport, a short unpaved road provides access to the Youghiogheny River, now dammed. When lake levels are low, the stone abutments of a former bridge that carried Old Morgantown Road over the Youghiogheny River are visible. A good overview of the area can be seen from the Maryland Welcome Center just east on I-68. Few people passing this area have any idea that a War of 1812 political fracas took place near here in November 1812.

HARFORD COUNTY

The Lay of Scottish Fiddle: A Tale of Havre de Grace

Nearly everyone has heard or even tried to say the tongue-twister "Peter Piper picked a peck of pickled peppers," but how many Marylanders know that the author of this well-known tongue-twister also wrote a satirical poem about the British destruction of Havre de Grace during the War of 1812? "The Lay of Scottish Fiddle: A Tale of Havre de Grace," was written in 1813 by James Kirke Paulding (1778–1860).[153] In it, Paulding wrote the following verse:

Childe Cockburn carried in his hand,
A rocket and a burning brand.
And waving o'er his august head,
The red-cross standard proudly spread.
Whence hung by silver tonsil fair,
A bloody scalp of human hair.

A parody of Sir Walter Scott's "Lay of the Last Minstrel," Paulding's "The Lay of the Scottish Fiddle" appeared anonymously, as had most of his earlier writings. This poem satires the predatory warfare of the British on Chesapeake Bay. Remarkably, it was published in London with a preface highly complementary to the author. The hero is Rear Admiral George Cockburn, and the principal incident is the burning and sacking of the little town of Havre de Grace. The poem provoked a fierce review from the *London Quarterly*. One reviewer called it "clever as a parody and contains many passages entirely original and of no inconsiderable beauty."[154] Paulding went on to become secretary of the navy from 1838–41. Who would have thought Peter Piper and Havre de Grace had anything in common?

Did Fifteen-Year-Old Matilda Succeed in Freeing Her Father from British Hands?

When four hundred British troops attacked Havre de Grace at dawn on May 3, 1813, Irish-born John O'Neill became a hero after nearly single-handedly attempting to defend the village. Following is his account of the incident:

We were attacked by fifteen English barges at break of day. We had a small breastwork erected, with two six and one nine-pounder[*] in it, and I was stationed at one of the guns. When the alarm was given, I ran to the battery and found but one man there, and two or three came afterwards. After firing a few shots, they retreated and left me alone in the battery. The grape-shot flew very thick about me. I loaded the gun myself, without any one to serve the vent, which you know is very dangerous, and fired her, when she recoiled and ran over my thigh. I retreated down to town and joined Mr. Barnes, of the nail manufactory, with a musket and fired on the barges while we had ammunition, and then retreated to the common, where I kept waving my hat to the militia who had run away to come to our assistance, but they proved cowardly and would not come back. At the same time, an English officer on horseback, followed by the marines, rode up and took me with two muskets in my hand. I was carried on board the Maidstone frigate, where I remained until released, three days since.[155]

Legend claims that John O'Neill's fifteen-year-old daughter Matilda successfully pleaded with Rear Admiral George Cockburn for the release of

Tortoiseshell box reportedly given to Matilda O'Neill by British Rear Admiral Cockburn when she pleaded for the release of her father. *Courtesy of Maryland Historical Society.*

her father after he was captured during the attack. For her bravery, Cockburn supposedly gave her a gold-mounted tortoise shell snuffbox, which can be seen at the Maryland Historical Society. Although the story is widely reported, actual documents indicate that O'Neill was released on parole upon application of the magistrates of Havre de Grace. One contemporary report indicated that a "Miss O'Neill" was among the town's committee members who visited the admiral under a flag of truce. Matilda may very well have pleaded for her father's release then and received the snuffbox, but if so, she was far from alone.

The legend is probably true, but most accounts suggest that Matilda went on her own to seek her father's release from the British. The actions of the town's committee may have been a result of the O'Neill family pleading for assistance—or the committee may have asked Matilda to come along to gain the sympathies of the British officers. We will never know for sure. Respect for John O'Neill can be gleaned from the tax roll of 1814, in which his entry was recorded by the assessor as a "list of property owned by the brave John O'Neal [*sic*]." This is the only known case in which the county assessor used this language. The city of Philadelphia presented John with a sword inscribed with the following: "Presented to the Gallant John O'Neil [*sic*] for his valor at Havre de Grace, by Philadelphia—1813."

Ralph Eshelman examined the supposed snuffbox at the Maryland Historical Society. It is lined inside with cloth and has no stains or odor to suggest it was ever used as a snuffbox. If this item indeed was presented to Matilda by Cockburn as token of his admiration for her bravery, it is a decorative box rather than a snuffbox, which would have been an unusual gift for a teenage girl. The legend of the snuffbox is so ingrained into the lore of Harford County that it is depicted on a silver entree dish contributed by the county in 1906 to the U.S. armed cruiser *Maryland*. It is exhibited with the rest of the *Maryland* silver service at the Maryland Statehouse.

PRINCE GEORGE'S COUNTY

Hunting Squirrels with Bayonets

During the British march toward Washington, D.C., in August 1814, before reaching their encampment at Nottingham, Lieutenant George Robert Gleig noticed what appeared to be a metallic reflection coming from the nearby woods. Below is his humorous account of the arrest of two Maryland militiamen published thirty-three years later:

> *I thought I could perceive something like the glitter of arms a little farther towards the middle of the wood. Sending several files of soldiers in different directions, I contrived to surround the spot, and then moving forward, I beheld two men dressed in black coats and armed with bright firelocks and bayonets, sitting under a tree; as soon as they observed me, they started up and took to their heels, but being hemmed in on all sides, they quickly perceived that to escape was impossible, and accordingly stood still. Having arrived within a few paces of where they stood, I heard the one say to the other, with a look of the most perfect simplicity, "Stop, John, till the gentlemen pass." There was something so ludicrous in this speech...that I could not help laughing aloud; nor was my mirth*

Two American militiamen surrounded by British soldiers plead that they were only hunting for squirrels. © *Gerry Embleton illustration.*

diminished by their attempts to persuade me that they were quiet country people, come out for no other purpose than to shoot squirrels. When I desired to know whether they carried bayonets to charge the squirrels as well as muskets to shoot them, they were rather at loss to a reply; but they grumbled exceedingly when they found themselves prisoners, and conducted as such to the column.[156]

ST. MARY'S COUNTY

Masthead Lanterns and Runaway Slaves

From August 5 to 27, 1813, the British established a base on Kent Island, on Maryland's Eastern Shore, for a naval and land assault on Queenstown (August 13) and St. Michaels (August 10 and 26). Soon afterward, on August 31, Rear Admiral George Cockburn abandoned Kent Island and sailed for Bermuda with his squadron of thirty-three ships. Left in command on the Chesapeake Bay was Captain Robert Barrie. His squadron of six ships, including his flagship, HM ship of the line* *Dragon*, were ordered to continue the blockade of the Chesapeake until Admiral Cockburn's return the following spring. Captain Barrie gathered his squadron near Point Lookout at the mouth of the Potomac River in St. Mary's County.

One of the British tactics was to encourage slaves to escape so as to create economic hardships for the plantation owners. Tobacco was a labor-intensive industry and without slaves, the "money crop" and their livelihood were threatened. The British would sometimes show a lantern in the mast of their ships to help the escaped slaves find them and freedom.

In late August, a barge from HM brig* *Mohawk* was sounding the shores at the mouth of St Jerome's Creek on the bay side six miles north of Point Lookout. An accompanying frigate,* either HM frigate *Conflict* or *Lacedemonian*, "kept a light at the mast-head, all night, supposed for the purpose of shewing [*sic*] the negroes the position of the ship for better facility in getting to her."[157]

One night, a negro slave and his wife from the Caleb Jones farm and another slave, Samuel Bean, escaped from their masters and boarded *Mohawk*. Caleb Jones, an ensign in the 12th Maryland Regiment of St. Mary's County, was surprised to find that on the night of August 25, his former slave had guided twelve or fifteen British soldiers to the farm. The ex-slave was "armed with a brace of pistols and a sword" and "treated his master very insolently."[158] This British raiding party took from the farm all six or seven of Jones's remaining slaves, as well as his livestock, house contents and several other slaves in the neighborhood. By mid-November, Captain Barrie made the following report:

> *The slaves continue to come off by every opportunity and I have now upwards of 120 men, women and children on board, I shall send about 50 of them to Bermuda in the Conflict. Among the slaves are several very intelligent fellows who are willing to act as local guides should their services be required in that way, and if their assertions be true, there is no doubt but the blacks of Virginia and Maryland would cheerfully take up arms and join us against the Americans.*[159]

The British plan to decimate the agricultural economy of the Chesapeake by welcoming slaves and ruining crops seemed to be working. While the light shining from the mast of a British vessel brought fear to many Americans, for others, it was a beacon for their escape to freedom. (See also "Escaped Slaves Serve as Colonial Marines Against Their Former Masters.")

OSWEGO, NEW YORK

Tent City Ruse

In addition to "The Eastern Neck Island Ruse," "The Big Annemessex River Stick Gun Ruse" and "The Corn Stalk Ruse at Mount Ephraim," there was another ruse, also by a Maryland Eastern Shore man. But this ruse took place not in Maryland but during the defense of Fort Oswego, New York, on May 5–6, 1814. Colonel George Edward Mitchell was a doctor who practiced at Elton, Cecil County. He served in the Maryland House of Delegates and on the state executive council. When war with Britain was certain, he accepted a commission in the U.S. Army on May 1, 1812, just weeks before war was officially declared. By 1814, he commanded the Third Artillery and faced a British fleet and more than a thousand attackers. Mitchell was brevetted* a colonel for his actions at Oswego.[160]

Replica War of 1812 tents from encampment reenactment. *Ralph Eshelman photograph.*

Mitchell realized that with less than four hundred men, he did not have sufficient troops to defend the fort, so he came up with a ruse. He ordered all the spare tents in storage to be pitched near the village to give the British a false sense of his strength. He then had two hundred militiamen* mingle around the tents in the village and in the nearby woods. Mitchell ordered his men to march from the fort back and forth several times to a forward position so that British observers would overestimate his force. He also ordered one company to infiltrate the woods near the ferry to give the impression that he was reinforcing the west side of the river. Mitchell believed his deception of placing tents in the village worked because when the British attacked, they advanced on what was his best-fortified position, leaving the village largely unmolested.[161]

Although legend claims that the ruse caused the British to call off their attack of Fort Oswego, in actuality, the British cannonaded* and then successfully captured the fort and barracks.[162] While the British could indeed claim victory, there was another important component to the battle that the Americans could claim. The British captured 2,400 barrels of useful supplies, including flour, pork, salt, bread and ordnance stores, as well as a few small schooners. But the British were unaware that twenty-one heavy cannons had not yet reached Fort Oswego and were still some eleven miles out at Oswego Falls (present-day Fulton, New York). Those much-needed guns eventually made it to Sackett's Harbor and were used to outfit ships that helped the United States control Lake Ontario for the rest of the war.

Virginia

Origin of "War Hawks"

War hawk, n (1798): one who clamors for war; esp: an American jingo favoring war with Britain around 1812.—Webster's Ninth New Collegiate Dictionary (1988)

The term "War Hawk" is often regarded as having been coined by the prominent Virginia congressman John Randolph, known as John Randolph of Roanoke, who ironically was a staunch opponent of war with England in 1812.[163] Was this term really coined by Randolph? An 1809 article in the *Annapolis Maryland Republican* suggests not:

> *"War Hawks" is a new coined name for the democratic* [-Republican] *party that promises to become current in the Federal papers. This is manufactured for the purpose of deceiving the people into the impression that the democrats have been desirous of provoking hostilities with England. The falsehood of which is notorious to any impartial or candid person who has observed the chain of measures pursued by Jefferson. How long and odiously was the Embargo supported, that we might thereby obtain justice without war. How explicitly did those few who offered to change that measure for more positive resistance to the aggressions of both France and England, declare that they resorted to it only through apprehension of civil war and disunion? How often was peace and intercourse invited? With what forbearance did we cling to peace? And with what sincerity did we reciprocate the olive when it came? Yet we are "war hawks" for maintaining those rights which we struggled for so long and so successfully, but which those peaceable lambs of federalism would have yielded at once to their much loved "mother Britain." "War Hawks."*[164]

John Randolph was one of the few Democratic-Republicans from the South and the western states who was anti-war. A review of the congressional debates in the 12th Congress of the United States, such as Randolph's own

Speech on the British War: House of Representatives of the United States, Washington, May 12, 1812 and similar debates, found no instances of Randolph's usage of the phrase "War Hawks." While Randolph is credited with having coined this phrase, there were several instances of the usage of the term in prewar newspaper articles, none attributed to Randolph. The following example is dated 1793:

> *M Genet's averment, that France does not expect America to join in the present European War, must operate as a death wound to the War Hawks who have lately been "whetting their beaks" in the would be Capitol of the United States.*[165]

Edmond Charles Genet (1763–1834) was a French minister who had arrived in the United States and was encouraging American privateers to attack British commercial vessels. President George Washington regarded these actions as a clear violation of American neutrality and demanded that France recall its minister. The Genet Affair, as it became known, led the Democratic-Republican party to cheer the triumphs of the French Revolution, while Alexander Hamilton, Secretary of the U.S. Treasury and one of the nation's founders, gave the opposite view.

Another example comes from an 1803 issue of the *Eastern Shore Republican Star*, which states, "War Hawks—the federalists are clamorous against the president [Jefferson] because he wishes to maintain union at home and peace abroad."[166]

The British impressment* of American seamen and the Orders in Council* had a disastrous effect on America's trade economy. The administrations of Presidents Jefferson (1801–09) and Madison (1809–17) sought economic trade restrictions to end these British acts but ultimately failed. A declaration of war soon became the cry from the influential politicians from the South and West. The "War Hawks" got their war, and anti-war U.S. congressman John Randolph was not the first to have used the phrase "War Hawks."

ACCOMACK COUNTY

Escaped Slaves Serve as Colonial Marines Against Their Former Masters

The British attacks on Chesapeake's plantation society created a challenge for the Americans. Vice Admiral Alexander Cochrane issued a proclamation offering slaves or free blacks service in His Majesty's armed forces or free passage to settle in nearby colonies. Slaves were fleeing from plantations in ever-increasing numbers. One hundred "Negroes" were reported to be on board HM ship of the line* *Dragon* at the end of April 1814.

The Americans, paranoid about slave rebellions, were both angry and frightened. They were in danger of losing their primary plantation labor force. Worse yet, some of the slaves were being converted into "troops, vindictive and capricious with a most reliable knowledge of every bye path."

Something was indeed happening that plantation owners could hardly imagine. Slaves were not only running away into the arms of the British, they were coming back to attack their former owners. At least seven hundred slaves—men, women, and children—were given shelter on Tangier Island (see "Reverend Thomas's 'Thou Shall Not Kill' Sermon" for more information on Tangier). As many as two hundred were being trained and issued arms to fight side by side with the British troops as a Colonial Corps of Marines (black marines whom the British often called "Ethiopians").[167]

The Battle of Pungoteague took place off Pocomoke Sound, southwest of Onancock on Virginia's Eastern Shore, on May 30, 1814. Here about thirty Colonial Marines with approximately five hundred British troops entered into Pungoteague Creek. The militia,* who occupied two barracks near the entrance to the creek, could not effectively fire on the British when they landed on the opposite side of the creek because their gunpowder was so poor. Some militiamen assembled on the opposite shore and soon came under fire from British cannons and Congreve Rockets.* The Americans returned fire with a four-pounder* Revolutionary War cannon as the British troops rushed the American line. A general fire ensued upon both sides. The militia withdrew into the thick woods after spiking (disabling) their cannon. But when an additional one thousand militiamen arrived, the British withdrew. At least six British troops were killed, including one member of the

Escaped slaves become Colonial Marines. *Artwork by Don Troiani. Research by James L. Kochan. Courtesy of Historical Art Prints.*

Colonial Marines. No Americans were killed, although two were wounded. An American militia officer described the action:

> *The enemy used his 18-lb., 12-lb., 4-lb. cannister and grape shot and Congreve Rocketts* [sic] *with great profusion but without effect. He soon landed from eight barges and Launches…and gave three cheers; put about 30 negroes* [Colonial Marines] *in full uniform in front and rushed upon the Major, receiving and giving a continued fire.*[168]

Rear Admiral George Cockburn reported to Vice Admiral Cochrane on the conduct of his newly trained recruits: "The conduct of our new raided corps, the Colonial Marines, who were for the first time, employed in arms against their old masters on this occassion [sic], and behaved to the admiration of every body."[169]

The Battle of Pungoteague was the largest engagement of the war on the Virginia Eastern Shore. The Americans had prevailed for a change, but this incident signaled a new and important factor in this all-too-familiar British policy of raiding: for the first time, they used their Colonial Corps of Marines. The Colonial Marines fought in many engagements in the Chesapeake, including in Virginia at Chesconessex, Farnham Church and Tappahannock and in Maryland at Benedict, Bladensburg, Lower Marlboro and North Point. (See also "Masthead Lanterns and Runaway Slaves.")

Reverend Thomas's "Thou Shall Not Kill" Sermon

One of the more unusual stories of the Eastern Shore during the War of 1812 originated on Tangier Island, in the Virginia waters of the Chesapeake Bay. This story became popular in 1861 with the publication of Reverend Adam Wallace's *The Parson of the Islands*, a biography of the Reverend Joshua Thomas, a Marylander who helped spread Methodism along the Eastern Shore of the Chesapeake Bay.[170] In this account, Wallace includes excerpts about the British occupation of Tangier Island and a prophetic sermon said to have been given by Thomas to the British troops before they embarked their ships to attack Baltimore. Tradition holds that the British officers on the island bestowed on Thomas the title of "Parson of the Islands."

Born at Potato Neck (now Fairmount), Somerset County, Maryland, Joshua Thomas (1775–1853), like most of the young men in this region,

Non-contemporary illustration depicting Reverend Joshua Thomas preaching to the British troops on Tangier Island in 1814. Taken from *The Parson of the Islands, 1861.*

became a waterman.* He was often called upon by the Reverend Joshua Reese to take him to the islands when Reese was summoned to preach. It was during these trips that Thomas became interested in organized religion. One of the principal places where he began to worship was along the Big Annemessex River where St. Peter's Methodist Church still stands, near Crisfield, Somerset County. It was here that Joshua Thomas gave his first sermon, converted to Methodism in 1807 and launched his log canoe* *The Methodist,* which he used to spread Methodism among the Eastern Shore islands. "Brother" Thomas was living on Tangier Island during the War of 1812 when the British occupied it as their main base of operations. Thomas described the British occupation as follows:

> *The first we knew of the British being nigh us was the report of their guns firing down the bay. The same day, some of their shipping came up abreast of my house and anchored. Soon after, we saw about fifty men in full uniform, with their weapons of war, land on the beach and proceed in marching order toward Z. [Zachariah] Crockett's house. Our women and*

children were dreadfully scared. They [the British] *remained on shore that night; and, after breakfast in the morning, went on board their ships; taking a lot of our cattle, sheep, and hogs with them, for which they paid such prices as they saw proper. They next…sailed away out of sight, and we saw no more of them for several days.*

In a short time, we heard their firing again, and four large ships appeared coming in. They cast anchor in Tangier Harbor and landed about two hundred men on the lower beach, where they pitched their tents and immediately went to work with all their might, clearing of the ground and building forts… and when they were finished, it was a most beautiful place. The two forts [redoubts] were erected a little to the south of the camp ground, east and west from each other, and about three hundred yards apart. The tents of the army were pitched in a semicircular form, extending about half round on the north side, and a very pleasant summer house was built in the center.[171]

The British encampment was near where the islanders established their campground among a beautiful grove of trees. In the summer, people from all around gathered here to worship and hear sermons by the reverend. It was considered sacred ground, and Thomas pleaded with the British officers not to damage the grounds—"the very gates of Heaven." When a Royal Marine cut down one of the trees, he was supposedly "given 30 days in imprisonment" by the British officers.[172]

Before the British departure to attack Baltimore in September 1814, Thomas gave his "Thou Shall Not Kill" sermon and predicted that the British would fail in their attempt to take the city. Thomas described the scene as follows:

Towards the close of summer, in the year 1814, we were made aware of some important movement among the forces encamped on the island. Preparations began both on shore and through the fleet in the harbor. Signals were exchanged, orders given, and all became bustle and activity. Before they left Tangier, they sent me word to be ready to hold a public meeting, and exhort the soldiers, on the campground. It was arranged to be on the last Sunday they were in camp. Early that morning, the flags were hoisted, the drums beat, and every preparation was made for a full turn out. Boats were plying from the ships to the shore, and bands of music were playing on board. At the hour appointed, the soldiers were all drawn up in solid columns, about twelve thousand men, under the pines of the old campground, which formed the open space in the centre of their tents.

I stood on a little platform erected at the end of the camp nearest the shore, all the men facing me with their hats off, and held by the right hand under the left arm. An officer stood on my right and one on my left, and sentries were stationed a little distance to the rear. After singing and prayer…I warned them of the danger and distress they would bring upon themselves and others by going to Baltimore with the object they had in view. I told them of the great wickedness of war and that God said, "Thou shalt not kill!" If you do, he will judge you at the last day; or, before then, he will cause you to "perish by the sword." I told them it was given me from the Almighty that they could not take Baltimore and would not succeed in their expedition. I exhorted them to prepare for death, for many of them would in all likelihood die soon, and I should see them no more till we met on the sound of the great trumpet before our final Judge.

Reverend Thomas claimed that the islanders could hear the booming of cannons as it "wafted o'er the waters." When the British returned to Tangier after the battle, he went to the beach to meet them. He was told that "hundreds of our brave men have been slain, and our best General [Robert Ross] is killed. It turned out just as you told us the Sunday before we left."[173] The British abandoned their base in February 1815 and left the Chesapeake never to return to Tangier. Peace was brought to the island once more, and Reverend Thomas was now a celebrated figure. The next camp meeting brought hundreds who had never before visited the island.

Joshua Thomas lived on Tangier Island until he was nearly fifty, when he and his family moved to Deal Island, Somerset County, Maryland. Here he and his parishioners built a chapel named for him. As the congregation grew, a larger church building was constructed. Thomas died on October 8, 1853, at the age of seventy-seven. He lies buried beneath a gravestone located at the south corner near the entrance of the Joshua Thomas Chapel. It is said that he wanted to be able to hear the sermon from his chapel each Sunday.

During World War II, the United States Maritime Commission christened the 178th Liberty Ship the USS *Joshua Thomas*, built by the Bethlehem-Fairfield Shipyard in Baltimore. During the United States Bicentennial celebration in 1976, Dr. Gerald Muller, professor and chairman of the Department of Music at Montgomery College, Rockville Campus, composed and produced an opera about the life of Reverend Joshua Thomas.

As with so many of these stories, no contemporary accounts of Reverend Thomas's famous sermon have been found. Wallace's account was the third—and only successful—attempt to write a biography of Thomas, Reverend Levin M. Prettyman and Reverend A. Manship having made two earlier attempts that were never finished. From Wallace's preface to *The Parson of the Islands*, it is clear that he depended for the most part on the "Prettyman Papers" that included a "manuscript narrative" from Thomas's birth up to 1815. What seems clear is that all of these attempts to write biographies depended largely on memories of Thomas rather than letters or other writings of the man himself. Apparently, Wallace, Prettyman and Manship wrote words they either remembered or believed Thomas might have said.

The information we have about Thomas is based on memory, much of it having come from stories Thomas told in his later years. How accurate these memories and stories are can only be speculated. Did Thomas actually speak before twelve thousand British troops? There were fewer than six thousand land troops who attacked Baltimore at North Point. With the crews of the British fleet included, perhaps a total of twelve thousand men was possible, but as with most stories, the numbers were probably inflated either by Thomas himself or his biographers, who wanted to cast Thomas in a most favorable light. It is probable that Thomas did give a sermon to the British at Tangier, but the facts behind the story are unclear and unsubstantiated. We will probably never know the full story of the "Parson of the Islands," but his legacy lives on, and his chapel and grave still survive on Deal Island.

ALBEMARLE COUNTY

Did President Jefferson Disrespect the Cockade City U.S. Volunteers?

The Petersburg Volunteers were raised in September 1812 under an act of February 1812. The number of men serving in the U.S. Army at the time was insufficient to adequately protect the American borders, let alone attack the British and their allies. Among the first recruits were the Petersburg U.S. Volunteers, who served at Fort Meigs, Ohio, in 1813. They were present at

Cast-iron fence surrounding the obelisk of Captain Richard McRae, commander of the Petersburg U.S. Volunteers. Note the cockade hat, musket, crossed swords and cartridge box incorporated into the design. *Ralph Eshelman photograph.*

the siege of Fort Meigs in May and June 1813 and remained in service until October 1813.

This volunteer unit was organized during a public meeting held at the Petersburg courthouse on September 8, 1812. A committee of eleven was appointed to raise funds by public subscription to finance the creation of the unit. The following resolution was adopted:

> *That the town of Petersburg will ever hold in high remembrance those Noble & Patriotic young men, who, unmindful of every other consideration, save love of country, have volunteered their services to retrieve the reputation of the republic, so shamefully, ignominiously and disgracefully sullied by the imbecile (if not treacherous) conduct of General Hull* [referring to Brigadier General William Hull, commander of the "North Western Army" who was bluffed into surrendering Detroit on August 16, 1812].[174]

The volunteers were described in a local newspaper as "not the dregs of society, culled from the by-lanes [and] alleys of the town; but of the flower of our youth and the best blood of our country…they have left the caresses of friends and the soft repose of their private life to tread the snows of Canada and the inhospitable wilds of the Savage."[175]

On October 21, 1812, the volunteers assembled at Centre Hill (the old historic section of Petersburg on the hill above the Appomattox River near Courthouse Avenue and Adams Street). There, Benjamin Watkins Leigh presented a flag made by the "fair hands" (women) of Petersburg. En route to Canada via Richmond, they were followed by carriages filled with ladies. The volunteers marched down Sycamore Street and across the Pocahontas Bridge over the Appomattox River, where a small cannon saluted them from a schooner.

The Petersburg U.S. Volunteers stopped at Monticello in the fall of 1812 on their way to Fort Meigs. Many accounts claim that the entire company was entertained by Thomas Jefferson.[176] However, other Federalist newspaper accounts differ.[177]

We drew up, in military array, at the base of the hill on which the great house [Monticello] was erected. About half way down the hill stood a very homely old man, dressed in plain Virginia cloth, his head uncovered and his venerable locks flowing in the wind. But how we were astonished when he advanced to our officers and introduced himself as Thomas Jefferson! The officers were invited in to a collation, while we were marched off to the town, where more abundant provisions had been made.[178]

As a singular instance of the small reliance that can be put…on newspaper paragraphs, I here subscribe an extract from my son's letter, who joined the Petersburg Volunteers. We…went three miles out of our way to gratify Mr. Jefferson's curiosity; and our expectations were highly raised, for we all expected to see and partake of every thing the house could afford, as having met the most bountiful treatment elsewhere; but we were all disappointed and horrified; though hungry, thirsty and tired, we got neither meat nor drink; not even water. We had a distant view of Mr. Jefferson and house.[179]

Jefferson sent them away without help, insulting them horrendously. This, while he keeps some British prisoners of war at his house as they eat and carouse free and far from war.[180]

These inexplicable contrasting accounts illustrate how one version alone does not necessarily provide the true measure of an event. The first account was published in 1862, fifty years after the event, and it could be argued that it does not reflect the true sentiment of the time of the event even though it supposedly quotes an earlier written letter. The last two accounts were published in 1812 and 1813, respectively, by an anti-war Federalist newspaper. The editor was no doubt biased in his regard to Jefferson and the U.S. Volunteers. It is hard to imagine a former president not showing respect for his fellow patriots. Perhaps Jefferson knew it was the intent for him to host the officers and the town the remaining volunteers. It is understandable that the volunteers might have become indignant that their officers were invited to Jefferson's home and they were not, not realizing appropriate fare was waiting for them in nearby Charlottesville. More likely, these accounts illustrate the differences in opinion of Jefferson and the politics of the time.

Petersburg is reputed to have been named the "Cockade City of the Union" by President James Madison when the Petersburg Volunteers visited Washington during their return from Fort Meigs, where they had distinguished themselves in 1813. Their leather cockade hats supposedly prompted President Madison to make the statement. In reality, the Petersburg Volunteers returned in several groups taking many different routes to Petersburg, although some soldiers may have stopped in Washington. The sobriquet may have been conferred when Captain Richard McRae, the unit's commander, visited Washington in July 1814. However, the appellation the "Cockade of the Union" seems to have first appeared in a toast on July 4, 1838, later showing up several times in the press between 1843 and 1848. The term "Cockade City" does not appear until after 1850. The Cockade Monument, also known as the Petersburg Volunteers Monument, located in Old Blandford Church Cemetery, is inscribed "Cockade City of the Union," but it was not erected until 1857. Thus, it is unclear who coined the phrase or when it was first used.[181]

ALEXANDRIA

Thanks to a Neck Scarf, a Midshipman Escapes Abduction

In order to keep the undefended city of Alexandria from being plundered or possibly burned by a British squadron approaching up the Potomac River, members of the city council reluctantly decided to surrender their city. The council accepted the British terms of capitulation, and British naval forces occupied Alexandria from August 28 through September 3, 1814. In exchange for the acceptance of these terms, the British agreed not to invade private dwellings or to molest the citizens of Alexandria. The British did, however, carry away as prizes three ships, four brigs,* ten schooners and three sloops.* They burned one partially sunken ship that they could not raise and captured a gunboat* from the Washington Navy Yard that had been sent to Alexandria for safekeeping. The British confiscated about 16,000 barrels of flour, about 1,000 hogsheads* of tobacco, 150 bales of cotton, as well as wine, sugar and other goods amounting to more than $5,000 in value. Alexandria mayor Charles Simms stated, "It is impossible that men could behave better than the Brittish [sic] behaved while the town was in their power, not a single inhabitant was insulted or injured by them in their person or houses."[182]

During the British occupation, U.S. Naval captains David Porter Jr. and John O. Creighton and Lieutenant Charles T. Platt reportedly put on civilian clothing to reconnoiter the town. At a warehouse near the intersection of Princess and Union Streets, they spotted a young British midshipman, John West Fraser, and a squad of men rolling out barrels of flour. One of them (many accounts claim Porter, but it is unclear which officer actually carried out the attempt) grabbed Fraser by his neck scarf and would have abducted him had the scarf not given way. Following are British and American accounts of the attempted kidnapping incident.

BRITISH VERSION:

An enterprising [American] *midshipman thought it would be fine fun to carry off an officer; and …dashed into the town on horseback…came boldly down to the boats, and seized a midshipman* [lieutenant] *by the*

A U.S. naval officer attempts to abduct British midshipman John West Fraser from the streets of Alexandria. © *Gerry Embleton illustration.*

collar. The fellow was strong and attempted to get him on his horse. The youngster, quite astonished, kicked and squalled most lustily; and after being dragged a hundred yards, the American was obliged to drop his brother officer. This operation…created a considerable alarm; the men retreated to the boats and prepared their carronades,* and were with difficulty prevented from firing. This occurrence soon found its way to the mayor, who came off in great alarm for the town. Captain [James Alexander] Gordon, with great good humour, admitted his apology and treated it…as a midshipman's spree; but recommended that proper precautions should be taken as a repetition…might lead to the destruction of the town.[183]

AMERICAN VERSION:

Capt. [David] *Porter, Lieutenant* [Master Commandant John O.] *Creighton and Lieutenant* [Midshipman Charles T.] *Platt naval officers rode into town like Saracens and seized on a poor unarmed Midshipman* [John Fraser], *a mere strapling, and would have carried him off or killd* [sic] *him had not his neck handerchief* [sic] *broke. This rash act excited the greatest alarm among the inhabitants of the town, women and children runing* [sic] *and screaming through the streets and hundreds of them layed* [sic] *out that night without shelter. I immediately prepared a message to Commodore* [Captain James Alexander Gordon] *explaining the manner and circumstances of this insult and sent it on board. While I was preparing the message, one of the Captains* [probably Captain Charles Napier] *rushed into the parlour* [sic] *with the strongest expressions of rage in his countenance, bringing with him the midshipman who had been so valiantly assaulted by those Gallant Naval Officers. I explained to him by whom the outrage was committed that the town had no control over them and ought not be held responsible for their conduct, and I was at that time preparing a message of explanation to the Commodore he said it was necessary that it should be explained, after which his fury seemd* [sic] *to abate and he went off, before Mr. Swann* [attorney] *and Mr. Lee* [former member of the Alexandria Common Council] *got on board the signal of battle was hoisted and all the vessels were prepared for action when Mr. Swann and Mr. Lee made their explanation & the Commodore said he was satisfied and ordered the signal of battle to be annulld* [sic], *thus the town was providentially preserved from destruction by the accidental circumstance of the midshipman's neck handkercief* [sic] *giving way, for had he been killd* [sic] *or carried off, I do not believe the town could have been saved from destruction.*[184]

Had the American officer succeeded in kidnapping the young British midshipman, it is very possible that Alexandria might have suffered the destruction similar to that which occurred at Hampton, Havre de Grace, Fredericksburg and Georgetown. Luckily, a loosely tied neck scarf gave way and possibly saved the day for Alexandria and its citizens.

FREDERICK COUNTY

Boyle's Reward for the Head or Ears of Rear Admiral Cockburn

With the British blockade of the Chesapeake and enemy troops raiding and plundering at will, citizens of the tidewater found a perfect villain on whom to take out their frustrations in the form of the hated British Rear Admiral George Cockburn. American newspapers printed venomous attacks against him. Cockburn was called the "Great Bandit" and the "Leader of a Host of Barbarians." A Baltimore newspaper published notice of a reward by a Virginian "naturalized Irishman" named James O. Boyle, who offered $1,000 for the head of the "violator of all laws, human [and] divine" or "five hundred dollars for each of his ears, on delivery."[185]

In reality, Rear Admiral Cockburn was an impressive and commanding flesh-and-blood counterpart of the Royal Navy's famous fictional contemporary heroes Jack Aubrey and Horatio Hornblower. Born to a London baronet, he was at sea as a midshipman while still a boy. He was fearless, capable and coldblooded—a combination that served him well in the fighting navy of Admiral Horatio Nelson. By the time he sailed to America in 1813 as a rear admiral, Cockburn was a seasoned veteran who had won the praise of the British House of Commons.

Americans only came close to collecting Rear Admiral Cockburn's head or his ears when his horse was shot from under him near the U.S. Capitol. After his Chesapeake service, he was chosen to transport Napoleon to his final exile on St. Helena in 1815. He capped his career as Admiral of the British Fleet and First Sea Lord. After a busy lifetime of seaborne adventures in harm's way, Sir George Cockburn died in his bed at the age of eighty-one.[186]

402   THE WEEKLY REGISTER—

which, they said, they were carrying to *market* when captured!—A day or two before, the Nymphe had *captured* a coasting vessel laden with live bullocks! Well may the "friends of commerce" bawl at Mr. *Madison,* "for cutting off the little *trade* that was left us," by his orders through the war and navy departments.

Mr. James M. Ludlum, of the city of New-York, has obtained letters patent from the United States, for a shot called "Tumbulated Cylinder Shot." It has been shown to several scientific gentlemen, who consider it ingenious, and believe it will have the desired effect, and if so, it certainly will be a great improvement to the art of warfare.

Too much British.—A certain *James O. Boyle,* a "naturalized Irishman," as he calls himself, residing at *Pugh town,* Va. offers a reward of *one thousand* dollars for the head of "the notorious incendiary and infamous scoundrel, and violator all laws, human and divine, the British admiral COCKBURN—or, *five hundred* dollars for each of his ears, on delivery." I do not know what Mr. O. Boyle could make of the ears of *Cockburn* to requite the expenditure. Brig. gen. *Proctor,* who has more experience in the value of *head-skins* than any one else, only gives *six* dollars for a whole scalp. Perhaps, as commodore *Chauncey* brought away the trophy suspended in the legislative hall of *Upper Canada* (the *scalp of a female)* Mr. O. Boyle designs to supply its loss with *ears of a monster.*

Newspaper ad offering reward of $1,000 for Admiral Cockburn's head or $500 for each of his ears. *Courtesy of Maryland State Archives.*

British Rear Admiral George Cockburn stands before his handiwork, an embellished version of the burning of Washington in 1814. *Courtesy of National Maritime Museum, Greenwich, England.*

HAMPTON

Did Frenchmen Fight Against the Americans in Virginia During the War of 1812?

It may surprise many, but yes, Frenchmen did fight against Americans in Virginia during the War of 1812. The British occupation of Hampton on June 25, 1813, was tainted by pillaging, murder and rape, most of which was believed to have been committed by members of two Companies of

Independent Foreigners who participated in the attacks at Craney Island (mouth of Elizabeth River) and Hampton. These companies consisted of French deserters and prisoners from the Peninsula War.* The British claimed that these men were spoiling for revenge for the loss of thirty Independent Foreigners during the Battle of Craney Island on June 22, 1813. Following is an American account of the plundering:

> *That the town and country adjacent was given up to the indiscriminate plunder of a licentious soldiery. In many houses not even a knife, a fork or a plate was left. The church was pillaged and the plate belonging to it was taken away. The wind-mills in the neighborhood were stript* [sic] *of their sails. The closets, private drawers and trunks of the inhabitants were broken open, and scarcely any thing semed* [sic] *to be too trifling an object to excite the cupidity of those robbers.*[187]

Here is an American account of atrocities blamed on the British but probably actually committed by the Independent Foreigners:

> *The enemy took possession of Hampton. During their stay, their conduct exhibited deeds of infamy and barbarity which none but British savages could have been so callous and lost to the tender feelings of human nature. They pillaged the place of every article they could convey…they murdered the sick and dying and committed the most hard and cruel insults to the defenseless young ladies. From such nefarious enemies good Lord deliver us is the prayer of your affectionate sister.*[188]

The British acknowledged the unacceptable behavior by the Independent Foreigners:

> *It is with great regret I am obliged to entreat your attention to the situation & conduct of the Two Independent Companies of Foreigners embarked on this service. Their behavior on the recent landing at Hampton…dispersing to plunder in every direction; their brutal treatment of several peaceable inhabitants, whose age or infirmities rendered them unable to get out of their way…and whose lives they threatened. I take the liberty of submitting to you the necessity of their being sent away as soon as possible.*[189]

American newspapers spread many stories of the atrocities committed during the British and Companies of Independent Foreigners occupation of

Hampton, but one story of the death of a very sick and aged man named Kirby, whose wife was shot in the hip and the family dog reportedly killed, is far from credible. Here are two newspaper accounts of the incident:

> *A Mr. Kilby* [sic], *near Hampton, was dying in his house in the arms of his wife when the British troops approached, and one of them cooly* [sic] *pulled out his pistol, shot poor Kilby* [sic] *and the ball lodged in the hip of the wife. "Expect no quarter," said an officer to his friend here.*[190]

> *Kirby, who for seven weeks or more had been confined to his bed, and whose death the savages only a little hastened, was shot in the arms of his wife… go to his wounded wife and hear her heart-rending tale.*[191]

Noted historian Benson J. Lossing visited this widow in 1853, forty years after the event. He wrote, "Her version of the story was that, with vengeful feelings, the soldiers chased an ugly dog into the house, which ran under Mr. Kirby's chair, in which he was sitting, and, in their eagerness to shoot the dog, shot the aged invalid, the bullet grazing the hip of Mrs. Kirby. Mrs. Kirby always considered the shooting of her husband an accident."[192] Thus, the shooting appears to be accidental, despite the claims of the contemporary American press. This is another example of biased newspaper reporting and rushed judgment in painting an account prejudiced by hatred of the enemy.

MATHEWS COUNTY (WITH VARIATIONS IN BALTIMORE AND CALVERT COUNTIES, MARYLAND)

Wasp Nest Captures a British Barge

The resemblance of a wasp's nest to a jug has resulted in a folktale reported from both Virginia and Maryland. The Virginia tale dates from at least 1898.[193] Sidney R. Riggin, collector of customs for the port of Crisfield, was known for an unusual ornament he kept in his home. The story holds that Riggin found the object in the woods—a "jug wasp" nest about a foot in length and diameter. Such nests are named for wasps that make nests resembling a jug. Riggin claims his father, William Riggin (1838–1905), told him a story about how such a nest captured a British gunboat.*

In 1812, a British gunboat* was lying near the shore of Matthews [sic] county, Va. A half-witted boy, who lived in that vicinity, found a nest of these papermakers one day, and, securely plugging up the entrances with mud, he cut the limb to which it adhered from the tree and carried the trophy on board to show it to the crew. The curiosity of the crew was at once excited and they wanted to know what it was. A "humming bird's nest," said the boy. "Don't you hear them inside?" The crew listened and could hear the indignant wasps keeping up a lively noise. The boy was invited below and, to show his goodwill, made the boat a present of the nest, cautioning the crew, however, not to let the birds out then, as they would follow him ashore. The crew waited until the boy had gained the shore, then they took out the plugs and the wasps at once proceeded to business. They never stopped work until they had made every one of the crew take to the water. The crew of the gunboat searched all over Matthews [sic] county for the boy, and his fate would have been bad, indeed, if they had captured him.

A 1907 magazine article about the British march on Baltimore mentions that one of the solders had noticed a peculiar nest hanging from a tree. Never having seen such a thing, he pierced it with his bayonet. However, the nest was not a wasp's nest but a hornet's nest, and the angry hornets promptly attacked him, causing him much discomfort. The stung soldier asked a nearby American, "Where did you get your d____ white-headed flies?"[194]

In 1941, a Southern Maryland newspaper published the same Virginia wasp story with a local twist. This time, as with 1907 account, the wasps were hornets, and the incident occurred at Lower Marlboro on the Patuxent River.[195] Here is the summarized story as told by "Uncle George" Younger:

The hornets surely won the day,
And made their foes feel shame;
These insects were American,
And lived up to their name.

The following Maryland version of the tale was discovered by Dr. Lucy Clausen and incorporated into her book on insect facts and lore published in 1954:

Sketch showing the North Point version of the wasps' nest story, in which a British soldier sticks his bayonet into the nest, causing them to attack. Elizabeth Franklin illustration taken from *Never Prod a Hornet: A Story about the War of 1812*.

In Maryland, they tell the story about a hornet's nest and the time a British vessel, said to have been a flagship, sailed up the Patuxent river during the War of 1812 and dropped anchor off Lower Marlboro. The officers went ashore to see something of the land of the Yankees. They were taking a walk through the woods and fields when they came upon a hornet's nest. Not knowing what it was, they called out to a young boy who was playing nearby and asked him. Recognizing the officers to be enemies of his country, the boy declared that the hornet's nest was actually the nest of a rare hummingbird and said: "If you stop up the hole at the bottom and take the nest out to sea, perhaps about ten miles, you will have a couple of little birds that will stay with the ship as mascots."

A short time later, the flagship weighed anchor and went down the Patuxent with the tide. What happened is still conjecture and report, although "Uncle George," who had told the story, never intimated that there was the slightest doubt about it. The plug must have been withdrawn according to the boy's directions because that day, about sunset, several of Lower Marlboro's residents, watching through glasses, saw Admiral Cockburn and a dozen of his officers dive overboard into the bay—swords and all![196]

This version of the story was repeated in a 1966 children's book about North Point during the War of 1812. Borrowing from the 1907 magazine article, in this version, the British ran a bayonet into the nest, causing the hornets to attack.[197] The story was repeated again in a 1983 children's booklet about the history of Lower Marlboro.[198]

The Virginia tale claims the nest was that of wasps, while the Maryland tale claims it was that of hornets. The Lower Marlboro version names a well-known British naval officer who had come up the Patuxent River, although his flagship was far down the Patuxent and not at Lower Marlboro. The tale is a myth but one of the more entertaining legends of the Chesapeake War of 1812.

NORFOLK

Cross-eyed Rooster Thief

During the war, Norfolk was considered a prime British target, so the port was defended by many militia* companies from around the state. One militiaman from Augusta County had a hankering for a rooster dinner, or as he put it, "for a fry of the feathered tribe." Knowing there were roosters on a nearby farm, he snuck over and took several, but before he could make his escape, an old woman at the farm saw the thief, who was distinguished by his crossed eyes. The next day, she reported the theft to one of the militia officers. Following is the reported conversation:

"Very well," responded the officer, *"come at eleven o'clock, when the company is mustered, and point him out to us."* She came at the appointed time. The Capt., not wishing to expose so respectable a man, told her to take a stand at the head of the company. She does so—the Capt. in front. *"Soldiers, eyes right!"* She then marched deliberately from right to left, and when she came to the extreme left, she pronounced them all cross-eyed! *"Well madam, we will reverse the order; eyes left!"* She marched back again, exclaiming ever and anon as she peered into the face of a soldier, *"D___n such a company—they are all cross-eyed!"*[199]

Could it be that the captain had partaken of the "fry of the feathered tribe" as well and thus did not want to betray the guilty soldier? This 1847 story is probably only meant to entertain and is not based on fact. (For a similarly entertaining but far-fetched Maryland tale, see "Carolinians Mistake the Talbot Militia for the British.")

VIRGINIA BEACH

British Capture "Hams, Mince Pies and Sausages, Leaving Not a Link Behind!"

Cape Henry, distinguished by the Cape Henry Lighthouse, completed in 1792, was an important landmark for the entrance of Chesapeake Bay. A British officer wrote of the lighthouse many years after the war, "The enemy, contrary to his own interest, (a rare occurrence with citizens of the United States,) had extinguished the light on Cape Henry: this gratuitous act saved us the trouble of 'dowsing the glim.'"[200]

The British conducted one of the first raids of the war on the Chesapeake at Cape Henry Lighthouse on February 14, 1813, taking meat from the lighthouse keeper's smokehouse. The raid was humorously described in the following newspaper account:

American newspapers ridiculed a British raid on Cape Henry Lighthouse when the raiders took meat from the keeper's smokehouse to supplement their bland rations. © *Gerry Embleton illustration.*

> *British valor and discipline. A band of veterans from Admiral* [John Borlase] *Warren's squadron landed at the lighthouse on Cape Henry and with the most undaunted heroism attacked the pantry and smokehouse of the keeper, captured his hams, mince pies and sausages, leaving not a link behind! After when, they effected their retreat in the greatest good order and regularity to their ships, with flying colors, without the loss of a ham! So much for British heroism and discipline—HUZZA! "England expects every man to do his duty!" This gallant and brilliant smokehouse exploit was achieved on the 14th inst.*[201]

This newspaper account is an example of American satire on the British. Humor aside, these British raids greatly impacted the economy and the lives of those living in the Chesapeake region.

Were Torpedoes Deployed Against the British?

In 1805, a commission recommended that the U.S. Navy support Robert Fulton's new invention, the torpedo. Most of us think of a torpedo as a self-propelled weapon with an explosive warhead that is launched above or below the water surface, propelled underwater toward a target and designed to detonate either on contact with its target or in proximity to it. But in the early nineteenth century, the term "torpedo" meant something very different. A torpedo then was a water mine. The British referred to these mines as "powder machines." In the summer of 1813, Secretary of the Navy William Jones encouraged Elijah Mix, who worked with Captain Charles Stewart of the U.S. frigate* *Constellation*, to use a torpedo in an attempt to blow up HM ship of the line* *Plantagenet* off the Chesapeake capes. During the night, Mix rowed near *Plantagenet* in an open boat named *Chesapeake's Revenge* and dropped a torpedo into the water, hoping it would drift into the vessel and explode. Despite several attempts, Mix was never successful, although on July 24, a torpedo exploded so near *Plantagenet* that it caused a cascade of water to fall on its deck. A newspaper account of the incident follows:

> *It was like the concussion of an earthquake attended with a sound louder and more terrific than the heaviest peal of thunder. A pyramid of water 50 feet in circumference was thrown up to the height of 30 or 40 feet... on ascending to its greatest height, it burst at the top with a tremendous explosion and fell in torrents on the deck of the ship, which rolled into the yawning chasm below.*[202]

Yes, torpedoes were used by the Americans against the British near the mouth of the Chesapeake Bay in 1813 and again in the Potomac River in 1814, but these attempts were unsuccessful and resulted only in British outrage of the use of such horrendous devices. Another torpedo attempt off New London, Connecticut, was more successful. There a torpedo blew up a small British vessel, inflicting a number of British casualties and increasing the acrimony between the two countries.

WESTMORELAND COUNTY
(WITH VARIATIONS IN BALTIMORE AND CHARLES COUNTIES, MARYLAND)

Poison Incidents

There are at least three accounts in the Chesapeake tidewater region of Americans attempting to poison British troops—two in Maryland and one in Virginia. Were these truly poison attempts? Let us examine all three.

During the British occupation of Benedict, Maryland, in June 1814, four barrels of poisoned whiskey were intentionally left for the British troops to drink. Below is an 1814 American newspaper account of the incident written by Clement Dorsey:

> *I heard with astonishment and indignation that a quantity of whiskey had been by design poisoned, by an infusion of arsenic, and left in the town* [Benedict]. *I considered the American character as deeply implicated in this horrible deed, so inconsistent with humanity and the established usages of nations that its immediate disclosure was called for, lest its effects might produce the intended design and thus give to our unfortunate situation a more desolating complexion. I determined immediately, under the sanction of a flag to return to the town, Dr. W*[illiam Hatch] *Dent and Mr.* [James] *Brawner attended me. We...met with the commanding officer* [Capt. Robert Barrie] [Dorsey having once previously talked with Barrie pleading to save the town from being burned]. *I have heard with astonishment that some person has most wickedly poisoned four barrels of whiskey* [Dr. Dent claimed only one barrel] *and left them here. I have done this upon my own responsibility. I shall communicate it to my government, if that approves of it, it will be to me consolation; if not, I have the approbation of my own breast.*[203]

It is heartening that Dr. William Hatch Dent, Clement Dorsey and James Brawner warned the British of this possible poisoning attempt. The fact that names are given and the newspaper account occurred only five days after the event suggests that this unfortunate incident actually occurred. It is interesting that in January 1813 Dorsey put up for sale a farm in the Benedict area that included a five-still distillery. Could the whiskey from this poisoning attempt have come from his own (or previously owned) still?

A second poison incident, or more likely a second version of the same incident, involved Charles Somerset Smith (1770–1831). British officers called at Mount Arundel (possibly Annarundel Mansion), Smith's home, also located at Benedict. The story goes that Smith hosted the officers by serving them wine, to which croton oil reportedly had been added. Croton oil is prepared from the seeds of *Croton tiglium*, also called purging croton or physic nut, which is derived from a tree native to or cultivated in India and the Malay Islands. When taken internally, even in minute doses, croton oil causes much colic and diarrhea. It is said that the officers became ill and remained at Benedict. Although some officers may have thought they had been poisoned, Smith would have been foolish to risk alienating his guests with such a trick. It is likely that this is a variant of the Benedict poison incident. It is also likely that some British officers had contracted one of the many ailments found in the Chesapeake during the "sickly season." Upon their return to Benedict after burning Washington, the British reputedly burned Mount Arundel.[204]

The next poison incident occurred a little over a month later in Virginia at Nomini Ferry, Westmoreland County. Soon after landing, a British officer discovered at the house of a Mrs. Thompson spirits set out with glasses all around. But because of the recent episode of poisoning at Benedict, Lieutenant James Scott kept his fellow comrades from sampling the whiskey. Below is his remembrance of the incident, published twenty years later in 1834:

> *The house* [Mrs. Thompson's]...*had evidently been their* [militia*] *headquarters. The largest room on the ground floor appeared as if it had been the scene of a carousing party, from the number of glasses, bottles of liquor, &c. that graced the whole length of the table. I fortunately observed that the glasses had not been used, and the full bottles created a painful suspicion that the wine and liquor might be poisoned, which, but for the recent transaction at Benedict, would not have crossed my mind...sent to the surgeon of the* [HM ship of the line*] *Albion for examination and found it to contain a very large quantity of arsenic.*[205]

While Lieutenant Scott claims that arsenic was discovered in at least one bottle, contemporary reports do not confirm his statement. Lieutenant Colonel Richard Elliott Parker (1783–1840) of the Virginia militia claims he "had drunk of the spirits but a few moments before the British came up, and that it was impossible it could have been poisoned."[206] Lieutenant Scott must have been mistaken in his memory, because the next day, Rear Admiral George Cockburn wrote a report to his superior:

> *It is perhaps right I should mention to you Sir that report was made to me, soon after landing at Nominy [sic], of an officer of the [H.M frigate*] Regulus having found a bottle of poisoned spirits set out in glasses round it in the porch of a house on the eminence we first gained, as however the officer unfortunately broke the bottle, it has been out of my power positively to ascertain the fact.[207]*

Lieutenant Colonel Parker stated, "The truth is, in her [Mrs. Thompson] hurry to get away, she had left some spirit and water in her porch, of which [Brigadier] General [John H.] Hungerford and myself, and the troops who attended us, drank afterwards."[208]

Although it appears that there was no poison, despite Lieutenant Scott's claim, the British burned Mrs. Thompson's house in retaliation for this assumed hideous act when "a negro had told somebody that some spirits, left on the table at a Mrs. Thompson, was poisoned."[209]

The last known incidents of poisoning occurred at North Point, Maryland, during the British landing on September 12, 1814, to attack Baltimore. Here is a British account of one incident:

> *Henry Dent a seaman…while looking for some hay for a bed he met a man in a drab colour coat with a pint bottle and asked him what it contained— told him it was spirits would he take some. Dent took the bottle and drank about a gill when some Marines making their appearance the stranger snatched the bottle from his mouth and ran hastily away into the wood close by. Dent came to me (he says in about half an hour after) in great pain and looking very ill. He stated the above circumstance and told me he thought himself poisoned by an American, he vomited a great deal, complained of pains in his head and belly, his eyes appeared much inflamed, he talked rationally, and I am certain was perfectly sober. I feel perfectly certain myself that the man had been poisoned.[210]*

A second reputed North Point poisoning incident claims that a slave by the name of Dick was left behind at the Trotton House (see "A Bag of Coins and Horse, Cart and Blankets" for another Trotten House tale). Here is an excerpt:

When news came that British were coming, Mrs. Trotten buried her silver in a cabbage patch in her garden. The family fled to Gatch's Mill; but the doctor had left behind his slaves and linements [sic], and his wife her homemade wines and cordials. Knowing the doctor's familiarity with drugs, the soldiers feared poison. They threw out all the medicines and compelled black Dick to sample all the wine before they would touch it. How long Dick remained sober, history does not say.[211]

The first North Point incident is supported by contemporary documentation, but the second incident has no such documentation and is therefore questionable. The latter incident was incorporated into a 1966 children's book about the War of 1812 in Patapsco Neck, Baltimore County.[212]

GREENBRIER COUNTY, WEST VIRGINIA

How Virginia Caves Helped the War Effort

Gunpowder was an important war material needed for the firing of cannons and small arms. Gunpowder mills were established in many locations in Virginia and Maryland, although the largest producer of gunpowder in the United States at the time was the E.I. du Pont Gunpowder Company near Wilmington, Delaware. Gunpowder, also known since the late nineteenth century as black powder, was the first and only chemical explosive known until the mid-1800s. It is made from a mixture of sulfur, charcoal and potassium nitrate (saltpetre or saltpeter). The sulfur and charcoal act as a fuel, while the saltpeter works as an oxidizer that contributes to the combustion of the powder. Readily soluble in water, saltpeter is found in some caves. Keep in mind that what today is West Virginia was Virginia during the War of 1812. Of the many Virginia caves that produced saltpeter, Organ Cave preserves an impressive thirty-seven saltpeter leaching hoppers (vats), including fragments of at least three that date from the War of 1812. The remaining hoppers are from the Civil War period. Saltpeter may have been mined here as early as the American Revolution, as the date 1704 is inscribed on the wall in a saltpeter producing area of the cave.

Scott Sheads looking at remains of Organ Cave War of 1812 saltpeter hopper. *Ralph Eshelman photograph.*

During the War of 1812, the market price for saltpeter was between seventy-five cents and one dollar per pound, making good saltpeter producing caves extremely valuable. An estimated 250 caves in the United States were mined during the American Revolution, the War of 1812 and the Civil War. During the War of 1812, saltpeter was mined from caves in Indiana, Kentucky, Tennessee and Virginia (including present-day West Virginia). Mammoth Cave, in Kentucky, is perhaps the best known. It is unclear exactly how many Maryland and Virginia caves were mined for saltpeter during the War of 1812, although Thomas Jefferson mentions that there were several caves in Virginia with saltpeter potential.[213]

Organ Cave is open for public tours, but the "1812 Room" can only be visited by making a strenuous guided "wild cave" tour, which involves much crawling. Only fragments of the original 1812 saltpeter hoppers survive. However, Civil War–era hoppers in excellent condition are visited on the public tour, giving one an idea of what the 1812 hoppers might have looked like. Tradition holds that the saltpeter was dragged by sled to the entrance of the cave and then shipped to the nearby town of Union, named so because it served as a rendezvous for troops during the Indian Wars. From there, it was probably transported to the du Pont Gunpowder Company, where gunpowder was made and then shipped to places like Fort McHenry. Few citizens of the Chesapeake area realize how important the saltpeter caves of Appalachia were to the war efforts during the American Revolutionary War, the War of 1812 and the Civil War.

Washington, D.C.

Who Burned the Anacostia Bridge?

In 1902, a newspaper published an article claiming that the Anacostia Bridge (present-day Pennsylvania Avenue) was burned by the British in 1814 after they left Washington, D.C. on their way to Baltimore.[214] The article below apparently had its origin during the fall of 1901, when some old piles were pulled out of the river.

> *People who live in the neighborhood of the ruins of the old bridge, and who during last fall had occasion to pull out some of the old piles, that for the most part are oak, found that that part of them which, through all the years since 1814, had remained under water, were almost as sound as the day they were put down. In summer, the piles of this ancient bridge are a favorite resort for small boys and fishermen, the former diving from the tops of these that stand the farthest above the water and the latter using them as a convenient place from which to fish. The marks of fire are discernible on the tops of some of them but at the best are very indistinct.*

There are several problems with this story. While it is possible that some of the wooden piles from the 1814 bridge survived the eighty-seven years since its burning, it is more likely that the piles are from a later rebuilding of the bridge. Evidence of fire described as "very indistinct" is not very convincing. Without dating the piles, it is impossible to be sure that these "relics" date from 1814.

More troubling is the claim that the British burned the bridge. The British did burn the Washington end of the long bridge to Alexandria (the Americans burned the Alexandria side), but it was the Americans who burned the lower two bridges over the Anacostia River to make it more difficult for the British to attack Washington. Ironically, the Americans did not burn the Bladensburg Bridge, where the British ultimately crossed the river. Finally, the British did not march from Washington to Baltimore. After occupying Washington, the British troops returned to their ships on the Patuxent River and then sailed to the Patapsco River to attack Baltimore. This 1902 newspaper article is a distortion of facts.

Who Burned Washington?

By 8:00 p.m. on the night of August 24, 1814, British troops had entered Washington. Only hours before, the Americans had been defeated on the fields of Bladensburg, and now the capital of the United States was occupied by the British army under the command of Major General Robert Ross. Beside Ross was Rear Admiral George Cockburn, commander of the naval forces. Together they led a contingent of their troops into the city and burned specific targets. Numerous accounts report that either the flames themselves or a red glow in the sky could be seen for miles around, in some accounts up to thirty-five miles away. Anyone seeing the glow or the flames was sure the city would soon be in ashes.

History books, documentaries and newspaper accounts all report that the British burned Washington during the War of 1812. A London newspaper exclaimed, "The Cossacks spared Paris, but we spared not the Capitol of America!"[215]

But did that really happen? Here are the facts. Washington City consisted of at least 350 structures in 1814. The British burned fewer than 20 of those structures, which is hardly the burning of the city that is so often claimed. Yes, the British burned important buildings, including the Capitol and the White House, but ironically, the American military actually burned as many if not more structures than did the British in an effort to keep military targets out of enemy hands and to make the British advance on Washington more difficult. Bridges and naval stores such as tar, hemp, cotton sails, rigging blocks, masts, spars and ships were all burned by the Americans. The British

Contemporary drawing showing the burning of the Washington Navy Yard, August 1814. *Courtesy of Library of Congress.*

burned public buildings as well as three private ropewalks.* The burning of the Washington Navy Yard and the ropewalks put up huge amounts of smoke and flame, which led many to believe that the entire city was burning.

HERE IS WHAT THE BRITISH BURNED:

- U.S. Capitol
- White House
- U.S. Arsenal at Greenleaf Point (scores of barrels of gunpowder and destruction of many cannons)
- U.S. Treasury
- Executive Office / War Office Building
- Belmont-Sewall House
- Three ropewalks
- Long Bridge over Potomac (one side burned by British, one side by Americans)
- A town house on Capitol Hill (believed to have been accidentally burned by sparks from the Capitol)
- Washington Navy Yard (any remaining targets after initial American burning)

HERE IS WHAT THE AMERICANS BURNED:

- Washington Navy Yard and storehouses (multiple buildings)
- U.S. frigate* *Columbia* (outfitted ready for sea)
- U.S. sloop* *Argus* (13 guns)
- U.S. frigate *Essex* (nearly ready for sea)
- Hull of U.S. frigate *Boston* (1799–1814, laid up in 1802 in ordinary)
- Hull of U.S. frigate *General Green* (1799–1814, laid up in 1802 in ordinary)
- Eastern Branch Lower Bridge
- Eastern Branch Bridge (not Bladensburg Bridge)
- Long Bridge over Potomac (one side burned by British, one side by Americans)
- Three barges
- Two gunboats*
- One row galley*
- Two hundred barrels of gunpowder

TOTAL ESTIMATED LOSS FROM AMERICAN BURNING: $678, 210[216]

Interestingly, the bridge the British used to cross the Eastern Branch (Anacostia River) at Bladensburg was not burned by the Americans (see "Who Burned the Anacostia Bridge?"). After the Americans burned most of the Navy Yard, the next day, the British burned anything remaining of military interest. It remains a mystery as to why the U.S. Marine Barracks, a logical British military target near the Navy Yard, was not burned.

The only known contemporary eyewitness drawing depicting the flames of the burning city actually shows the Navy Yard burning, not the city itself. The smoke and flames seen in the sky over Washington that night were as much caused by the Americans as by the British. It is not accurate to say that the British burned Washington; it is accurate to say that the British burned many of the public buildings, such as the Capitol and the White House, but even parts of these buildings survive today, some with scorch marks from that fateful fire (see "Was the President's House Painted White?").[217]

Speaker's Chair, Brothel and Dinner Light from Blazing Buildings

On the evening of August 24, 1814, the British marched into Washington after having defeated the Americans at Bladensburg. Numerous legends arose from their occupation of the capital city, and among them are several attributed to Rear Admiral George Cockburn, commander of the naval forces that accompanied Major General Robert Ross's army into the city. Upon entering the U.S. Capitol building, Cockburn is said to have occupied the speaker's chair and, in a mocking manner, asked the troops whether they should burn the Capitol building. That evening, while eating dinner at Suter's Tavern, he supposedly asked that a candle be taken away as he preferred to sup by the light of the nearby burning Federal buildings.

Did the admiral really stay in a brothel that night? What is the origin of such stories? There are no contemporary written accounts that support them. As best can be determined, this story and others like it may have become popularized from a Washington City Guide published in 1861 and picked up by an English journalist, George Augustus Sala (1828–95), who visited Washington and wrote about it in *My Diary In America in the Midst of War*, published in 1865.[218]

Sala's account is amusing, as it ridicules Americans for spreading these tall tales:

> [N]*eed I remind the historical student that at the door of the British nation lies the Vandalic* reproach of having destroyed the interior of both wings of the Capitol by fire. It was worthy of the blundering Administration with which England was then afflicted to send an army of Peninsular veterans* [Peninsula War*] *to burn the senate-house of a sucking Republic. The most accredited of English historians have admitted the wanton barbarism exhibited by the commanders of the British expeditionary force after the route of the raw American militia, known as the "Races of Bladensburg;" so the Tories, I trust, will not accuse me of falsifying history, in stigmatizing the destruction of the public buildings at Washington in 1814 as a stupid, brutal, and useless act. At the same time, the stories told by the Americans as to the behavior of our troops while in possession of Washington must be taken with a very large grain of salt…but it is assuredly incredible to be told that a gallant and high-minded officer and gentleman such as Admiral Cockburn undoubtedly…should have gratuitously insulted the inhabitants*

Admiral Cockburn in the speaker's chair at the Capitol. *Granger image.*

*of a captured town by "riding a switch-tail mare, accompanied by her foal"
down Pennsylvania Avenue…extinguishing the lights and eating his supper
by the light of the blazing buildings! Yet all this the Americans gravely tell a
stranger and have put upon the printed record. In the fashionable guide-book
to Washington and its vicinity, you may read that, when the Capitol was
seized, Admiral Cockburn entered the Senate, mounted the Speaker's chair,
and put the question, "Shall this harbor of Yankee democracy be burned?
All for it will say 'Ay,'"—truly a likely mode of speech for a British
seaman to make; and that, after reversing the question, he pronounced the
motion carried unanimously and ordered combustibles to be applied to the
hall. In another page of the same book, it is coolly asserted that "Admiral
Cockburn, with a few of his dissolute companions, spent the night in a*

brothel, rivalling [sic] *the elements in rendering the night hideous with disgusting orgies." War is generally looked upon as chiefly productive of bloodshed, misery, and pauperism; but here is another item in which it most fecund—to wit. Lies.*[219]

In his narrative, Sala gives a clue as to where he got these stories: "the fashionable guide-book to Washington and its vicinity." The same stories also appeared in an 1861 guide to Washington entitled *Philip's Washington Described: A Complete View of the American Capital.*[220] These are the earliest written accounts of these stories presently known. Unfortunately, no references are provided as to where Philip got the stories. The stories were subsequently repeated in 1869 and 1880 newspaper articles.[221]

None of these stories can be confirmed by any contemporary documentation, but there is one Cockburn story that is true. While Cockburn was in the Capitol, he entered the president's room and took President James Madison's personal ledger entitled RECTs & EXPENDs US FOR 1810 [Receipts & Expenditures for the U.S. 1810]. Its inscription, written by Cockburn himself, reads on the inside, "Taken in President's room in the Capitol, at the destruction of that building by the British, on the Capture of Washington 24th August 1814." The book was later returned to the U.S. government by a book dealer.

Who Really Saved George Washington's Portrait?

One of the most popular legends to have come out of the War of 1812 was that Dolley Madison saved the portrait of George Washington. This story stems from a letter she wrote to her sister Lucy Payne Todd:

I have ordered the frame to be broken, and the canvas taken out…the precious portrait placed in the hands of two gentlemen [Jacob Barker and Robert G.L. De Peyster] *of New York for safe keeping. And now, dear sister, I must leave this house or the retreating army will make me a prisoner in it by filling up the road I am directed to take. When I shall again write to you, or where I shall be tomorrow, I cannot tell!*[222]

Dolley Madison directing the removal of the George Washington portrait. *Courtesy of Montpelier Foundation.*

What most Americans don't realize is that Dolley's letter, as well as others of hers from this period, were lost. Dolley was later asked to re-create them for a biography as best as her memory could serve. Thus, the letter above was not written on August 24, 1814, but many years later.[223] Mrs. Madison wrote about the event again in 1848:

> *The impression that Mr. [Charles] Carroll [family friend] saved Stuart's portrait of Washington is erroneous. I have heard that his family believed he rescued it. On the contrary, Mr. Carroll had left me to join Mr. Madison, when I directed my servants in what manner to remove it from the wall, remaining with them until it was done. I saw Mr. Barker and yourself [De Peyster] passing and accepted your offer to assist me, in any way, by inviting you to help me to preserve this portrait, which you kindly carried, between you, to the humble but safe roof which sheltered it awhile. I acted thus because of my respect for General Washington—not that I felt a desire to gain laurels; but, should there be a merit in remaining an hour in danger of life and liberty to save the likeness of anything, the merit in this case belongs to me.[224]*

Is it likely that Mrs. Madison's memory was sound after thirty-four years? Might she have embellished the event? While we will never know for sure, there are at least two other accounts of this event.

Paul Jennings was a slave who served as President Madison's footman. He later recalled:

> *It has often been stated in print that when Mrs. Madison escaped from the White House, she cut out from the frame the large portrait of Washington… and carried it off. This is totally false. She had no time for doing it. It*

would have required a ladder to get it down. All she carried off was the silver in her reticule, as the British were...expected every moment.

Jennings said that Jean Pierre Sioussat, a steward, and Thomas McGraw, a gardener, actually removed the canvas "and sent it off on a wagon, with some large silver urns and such other valuables as could be hastily got hold of."[225]

Jacob Barker (1779–1871) wrote his own account in 1847, thirty-four years after the event. He states that the purpose of his narrative "is with the view of rendering to Mrs. Madison the credit to which she is justly entitled for the suggestion which led to the saving of this [Washington's] Portrait; and further, also, to show who assisted in carrying her wishes into effect. The merit which has been claimed by others virtually belongs to her."[226] Following is more from Barker's account:

On handing Mrs. Madison...into the carriage, Mrs. Madison said to me—"Mr. Barker, I wish you, if you cannot save, to destroy, the portrait of Gen. Washington...the portrait I am very anxious to save...at all events do not let them fall into the hands of the enemy." We immediately set about carrying into effect the directions of Mrs. Madison. We took the portrait; you [De Peyster] and I held each a corner of the light frame on which it was extended, having left the gilt frame on the floor of the room, my servant the third, and the hired black boy the other, and fell into the trail of the army, marched with them through Georgetown, and several miles on the road to Montgomery Court House. We were unable from fatigue to continue with the army and therefore turned off into the woods with the portrait. We were kindly received there at the residence of a widow lady. We arranged with our hostess to retain the portrait until one of us should call for it. Six weeks after the burning of Washington, I... visited the widow...found it in good condition, reclaimed it, compensated her for her trouble, took it back to Washington, and delivered it to the Secretary of State, who promised to have it varnished, placed in a frame, and reinstated in the President's house.

Barker felt compelled to write his account when somehow, "General Jackson" (presumably Andrew Jackson) and General John Mason were being given credit for having saved the Washington portrait.[227] Jackson was not even in Washington at that time. He was apparently being confused with General Mason, who was in Washington with the president. It is possible that Mason oversaw the revarnishing and even the rehanging of the portrait. This is an example of a how a well-known hero such as Jackson is brought into a story to save a national treasure in lieu of the circumstances and facts.

If Barker is correct in his narrative, Dolley had already left the White House before the portrait was even taken down from the wall. This is somewhat supported by Jennings, but his narrative is not as definitive. According to Mrs. Madison's account, she stayed until the painting was safely taken down from the wall. It is also interesting that at least three other individuals were given credit for having saved the Washington portrait: General (Andrew?) Jackson, General John Mason and family friend Charles Carroll.

Dolley certainly played a role in saving the portrait of the father of the United States, but she also had plenty of help. Dolley should get credit for suggesting the saving of the portrait, but the task itself was apparently left for others to accomplish. The painting was not cut out from the frame as many believe. When Barker returned the painting weeks later, the Madisons reportedly gave him a three-piece silver tea set in appreciation for his assistance. That set, later returned, is now among the treasures of the White House.

It is interesting that all three accounts were written many years after the event. As with many legends, we will never know the complete truth of what happened that afternoon, but certainly there were many who had roles in helping to save the George Washington portrait, which to this day hangs in the East Room of the White House.

Did the Great Storm Put Out the Flames of Washington?

We have already dispelled the legend that Washington City was burned by the British. In fact, only a small portion of the city was burned (see "Who Burned Washington?"). Did the great storm that arrived over Washington on the afternoon of August 25 actually put out the fires in the city and help to save it from further damage? The Washington Navy Yard, by order of the Secretary of the Navy William Jones, was set on fire by naval personnel about 8:00 p.m. on August 24, and the Capitol building was set on fire by the British about 9:00 p.m. that evening. The White House, U.S. Treasury building and the federal arsenal were set ablaze by the British about 11:00 p.m. The following morning, additional structures were burned, including the War Department building.

The great storm, a severe line of thunder squalls accompanied by ferocious winds, torrential rains and probably tornados, arrived about 2:00 p.m. on August 25.[228] By this time, the Capitol and Navy Yard had been on fire for about seventeen hours and the White House and U.S. Treasury building for about fifteen hours. It is likely that most of the combustibles in these structures had been consumed by this point, leaving only burned-out stone shells, smoldering ashes and smoke. The War Department building, torched that morning, might still have had flames, although much reduced from their initial strength.

By the time the storm arrived, the rains no doubt helped to extinguish the embers, but it is doubtful that there were still flames emanating from the Capitol and White House. While legend claims that the storm helped to put out the fires and save the city, the opposite actually occurred. The storm was so severe that it caused additional damage to the city, ripping off roofs as if they were made of matchsticks. The winds were so violent that they toppled three brick chimneys on the Patent Office and General Post Office. The chains on the drawbridge across the Potomac to Alexandria were buckled so that the draw could not be raised. Trees were uprooted, and some wooden houses were flattened by the force of the winds. For the Capitol and the White House, it was even worse. The stone walls, still retaining heat from the fire, splintered and spalled when soaked by the cold rains from the storm.[229] To add insult to injury, some citizens of the city began to pillage the government buildings as soon as they were abandoned. Furniture—even hinges and doorknobs—were stolen from the Navy Yard, and silver and other valuables were taken from the White House. Some of these treasures were later returned. The great storm did not help to save Washington—it only added to the destruction.

Was the President's House Painted White?

In the century following the War of 1812, a popular myth grew that the President's House had been painted white after the British burned it in 1814. But is this really true? The President's House, begun in 1792 and completed in 1802, was first occupied by President John Adams in November 1800. The British burned it about 11:00 p.m. on August 24, 1814, leaving a roofless stone shell.

Ralph Eshelman standing at the White House lower doorway near the kitchen and pointing to scorch marks on the sandstone arch. *Peter Stone photograph.*

When President James and First Lady Dolley Madison returned to the President's House after the British occupation of the capital, Madison was adamant that the house be restored as previously built. The original architect, James Hoban, was hired to supervise the reconstruction with only a few architectural changes. It was completed in 1817 under the administration of Madison's successor, James Monroe, Madison's former secretary of state and acting secretary of war during the War of 1812.

The White House is made of tan-colored Aquia sandstone quarried from Aquia Creek in Stafford County, Virginia. This stone was also used in other notable buildings in Washington, including the Capitol. According to some accounts, the original sandstone that survived the burning of 1814 was "white washed" or painted to hide scorch marks. However, whitewashing was a standard method of providing a protective coating, and the President's House was whitewashed as early as the fall of 1798, six years after being completed and sixteen years before the British burning. As early as 1810, the term "White House" was used in referring to the building.[230] Some accounts claim that George Washington named the mansion after the white house in which his wife, Martha Dandridge Custis, was living when he proposed to her. Since Washington died in 1799, the President's House would have had to be called the White House prior to 1810, but no such references are known. By the mid-nineteenth century, the structure had become known as the Executive Mansion. In 1901, President Theodore Roosevelt signed an order officially naming the building the "White House."

During exterior renovations in 1978–94, some thirty layers of paint and whitewash were removed. The carved sill under one first-floor window on the north front, immediately west of the North Portico, has been left unpainted to show the original stone color. Thus, while the White House was no doubt whitewashed and painted white after being rebuilt in 1817, it was sometimes called the "White House" prior to the war. The legend of painting the President's House white to hide scorch marks may be true, but it was not the reason the structure is called the White House. There are still places where the scorch marks are visible, never having been painted or whitewashed.

"An Ounce of British Influence": Commodore Barney's Musket Ball

On the afternoon of August 24, 1814, the British army defeated the American forces at the Battle of Bladensburg, opening the way for the invading British to capture the U.S. Capitol. This humiliating defeat at Bladensburg and subsequent burning of the Capitol and President's House in Washington were the low point of the War of 1812 for the Americans.

A rare point of pride at this time was the heroic resistance of the U.S. Navy flotilla men and the U.S. Marines commanded by Commodore Joshua Barney. Rear Admiral George Cockburn, a senior British officer at the Battle of Bladensburg, commented that Barney and his men "have given us the only fighting we have had."[231] Out-flanked, Barney ordered his men to retreat,

The British musket ball that ultimately took Commodore Barney's life. *Courtesy of the Daughters of the American Revolution, Washington, D.C.*

but not before he was wounded in the thigh. Faint and lying in a pool of his own blood, Barney was unable to escape the enemy and summoned a British soldier to seek an officer for him to speak to. Lieutenant James Scott, Cockburn's aide de camp, appeared and then sought out Cockburn, who soon arrived with Major General Robert Ross, the commander of the British invasion force. After introducing themselves and realizing who Barney was, the officers paroled Barney out of respect and conveyed him to a tavern in town where he received medical treatment. The musket ball, deeply lodged in his thigh, was not removed. His wife, Harriet, his eldest son, William Bedfort Barney, and Dr. Thomas Hamilton arrived on September 27 to accompany Barney to his home at Savage, Howard County, Maryland, to convalesce. Barney wrote to the Secretary of the Navy five days later:

> *Sir…My wound is deep, but I flatter myself not dangerous; the ball is not yet extracted. I fondly hope a few weeks will restore me to health and that an*

exchange will take place that I may resume my command, or any other that you and the President may think proper to honor me with. Yours respectfully, Joshua Barney.[232]

In 1818, four years later, Barney departed from his farm for Kentucky to look into some land dealings. As the commodore and his wife were preparing to leave, his son William leaned over to his father and in a half whisper so that he would not be heard by his mother asked that if the commodore should die before him that he bequeath to him the "ounce of British influence he had labored under, ever since the Battle of Bladensburg."[233] The old commodore and his wife had only made it to Pittsburgh before his health deteriorated into a bilious fever. It is believed that the long, arduous journey had caused his four-year-old wound to fester, causing his death on December 1, 1818. Barney was buried at Pittsburgh, far from the sea at which he had spent most of his service to his country.

Thus, it is likely that William had the musket ball mounted within a hole on a silver disk to be worn as a pendant in remembrance of his beloved father. On the disk are inscribed the following words: "This British bullet terminated the life of Commodore Joshua Barney in defending Washington." In 1919, Richard H. Thompson, a descendant of Barney, presented several Barney family heirlooms, including "the bullet, mounted in silver," to the Daughters of the American Revolution.[234]

A Musket Barrel Fence

In historic Georgetown, Washington, D.C., there is a handsome brick building surrounded on two sides by a fence made of musket barrels said to date from the Revolutionary War and the War of 1812. In the 1840s, gunsmith merchant Reuben Daw (1808–91) took advantage of available war surplus and obtained 364 musket barrels from the Washington Navy Yard. Daw had just finished the construction of a fine town house and garden in Georgetown and needed a fence at what today is P Street between Twenty-eighth and Twenty-ninth Streets.[235]

Daw cleverly used his government scrap metal to fabricate a fence using the musket barrels as pickets. By 1911, the house had fallen into ruins, but the rusted fence still remained. Today, the house has been restored, and the

Above: Gun barrel fence. Note the tapering of the barrels. *Ralph Eshelman photograph.*

Left: Detail of fence picket showing either gun sight or stud for bayonet attachment. *Ralph Eshelman photograph.*

fence is in good condition, although it has been covered with so many coats of paint that the details of the barrels are difficult to discern.

This story appears to be true. The musket barrels taper just as one would expect. The openings in the barrels are covered by decorative finials, so one cannot see the barrel end. Near the tip of some of the barrels can still be seen either gun sights or a stud for attachment of a bayonet. No markings on the barrels were found, but the numerous coats of paint may have masked any such markings. It seems more likely the musket barrels would have come from the U.S. Arsenal at Greenleaf Point in Washington as opposed to the Washington Navy Yard.

Endnotes

1. Quote from the 1962 American western film *The Man Who Shot Liberty Valance.*
2. Kessler, "The Fact Checker," *Washington Post*, December 16, 2012, A2.
3. Barden, *Virginia Folk Legends*, 2. Defines a legend as a "traditional prose narrative, set in this world [as opposed to the spirit world], in the past, involving human characters, which is regarded as fact by its teller and its audience."
4. Graves, "Why the White House Was Burned," 1095–1127.
5. Hickey, *Don't Give Up the Ship*, xx–xxi.
6. Jones, *Keene Family History*, 82.
7. Flowers, ed., *Dorchester Tercentenary*, 81. Polly was born Mary C. Dove on April 18, 1777. She married John Critchett Travers on April 5, 1797, and died in 1857. Some accounts give Mrs. Travers's name as Polly Dove.
8. See http://www.silvercollection.it/ENGLADIXON.html.
9. Bennett, *Never Prod A Hornet*, 31. Trotter is usually spelled Trotten in other sources.
10. "Historic Cannon Explodes," *The Sun*, November 14, 1912.
11. "Recalls Queer Battle," *The Sun*, July 12, 1909.
12. "Death of a Veteran," *Easton Gazette*, March 7, 1848.
13. "Battle of the Ice Mound," *American and Commercial Daily Advertiser*, February 22, 1815; Stewart, "The Battle of the Ice Mound," 372–78. Stewart's article includes a list of men who were in Joseph Stewart's report written after the engagement as well as the names of men who were to receive prize money from the capture and sale of the tender and its supplies.

14. "Caulk's Field Marker," *The Sun*, October 19, 1902.

15. Ibid.

16. A search of contemporary newspapers from the region failed to give any accounts of who fired the shot.

17. "Sketch of the Attack," National Archives UK, ADM 1/507.

18. Lieutenant Colonel Philip Reed to Brigadier General Benjamin Chambers, September 3, 1814. *Niles' Weekly Register*, September 3, 1814, vol. 7, 150.

19. *Baltimore Patriot*, September 5, 1814; *Federal Gazette and Baltimore Daily Advertiser*, September 7, 1814. The *Federal Gazette* reported the following based on a letter from Chestertown dated September 1, 1814: "Sir Peter received two wounds, the last of which was in the head and killed him instantaneously."

20. Carmack, *Your Guide to Cemetery Research*, 136; Smith, *Voices From the Cities of the Dead*, 80.

21. Beynon "A Journal Kept Aboard HMS *Menelaus*."

22. Barrett, *The 85th King's Light Infantry*, 167.

23. *Morning Mail*, May 15, 1815; "Remarks, &c., on board HMS *Albion*, October 14, 1814," George Cockburn Papers, Library of Congress, MSS 17576, reel 5, containers 7-8; Tucker, "Sir Peter Parker," 189–95.

24. "Proceedings of the Governor and Council," Maryland State Archives, SC 3159, 585. Joseph Mitchell was appointed contractor for the Kent County militia.

25. "Huzza for the Militia," *National Intelligencer*, September 5, 1814.

26. Beynon "A Journal kept Aboard HMS *Menelaus*."

27. Ibid.

28. Colonel Philip Reed to Major General Samuel Smith, September 18, 1814.

29. "Peter Parker's Cannon," *The Sun*, July 4, 1899.

30. Hemstock, "Quiet Monument Belied as Explosive Past," 13.

31. "Painful Accident," *The Sun*, July 11, 1843.

32. "Peter Parker's Cannon," *The Sun*, July 4, 1899.

33. Hemstock, "Quiet Monument Belied as Explosive Past," 13.

34. Rypka, "From the Archives of St. Paul"; Ford, "The Battle of St. Paul's Church Yard."

35. "Caulk's Field Marker," *The Sun*, October 19, 1902.

36. Barroll, "Remarks on General Philip Reed"; Captain Peter Parker to Vice Admiral Alexander Cochrane, August 29, 1814.

37. Knight's obituary as quoted in *The Sun*, August 10, 1913.

38. "Maryland Obituary, Mrs. Kinsey E. Thomas," *The Sun*, February 2, 1900.

39. "To the Editor of the *Republican Star*, May 23, 1814," *Republican Star*, May 31, 1814.

40. "Jacob Gibson," *Baltimore Federal Republican*, May 5, 1813; Hanks Jr., *Tales of Sharp's Island*, 4–10.

41. The two six-pounders were purchased from Isaac McKim of Baltimore, aide-de-camp to Major General Samuel Smith.

42. *Baltimore American*, April 17, 22, 1890. Thomas Kemp died April 16, 1890, at age ninety; "St. Michaels Defense," *Baltimore American*, September 6, 1897.

43. Ingraham, *Land of Legendary Lore*, 114.

44. Sewall, "Battle of St. Michaels," 6.

45. Ibid., 24–26.

46. Plummer, "Another Look at the Battle of St. Michaels," 10–17. This is the first in-depth study based on primary documents of the Battle of St. Michaels. Thomas Norton came to the same conclusion in an article he wrote for the May 16, 2005 issue of the Easton *Star Democrat*; Dawson, "Did St. Michaels Really Fool the British?" Based upon Kemp's 1890 recollection, Dawson believes the story is plausible, "although it is true there are no contemporary accounts."

47. Dawson, "Did St. Michaels Really Fool the British?"

48. Ibid.

49. Ibid.

50. Ingraham, *Land of Legendary Lore*, 114–15.

51. "The Town of Royal Oak," *The Sun*, April 14, 1907.

52. "A Relic of the War of 1812," *The Sun*, April 17, 1884.

53. "Death of the Royal Oak," *Easton Gazette*, July 31, 1858.

54. "Lines, Suggested by Reading an Account of the Death of the Royal Oak," *Easton Gazette*, August 14, 1858.

55. "Death of the Royal Oak," *Easton Gazette*, July 31, 1858.

56. "A Relic of the War of 1812," *The Sun*, April 17, 1884.

57. Dobbin, "A Shot That Named a Town," *The Sun*, July 30, 1961.

58. See http://genforum.genealogy.com/killman/messages/113.html.

59. "The Town of Royal Oak," *The Sun*, April 14, 1907.

60. Ibid.; "Royal Oak's Historic Relics," *The Sun*, May 12, 1885.

61. Additional information can be found at http://royaloakmd.org/tree.htm.

62. "Fort Stokes, Its History," *Easton Star*, February 19, 1861.

63. "Great Union Victory at Cow Landing," *Easton Star*, January 19, 1862. Sarcastically signed "Cow Landing," the original name of Easton Point.

64. Arnett, Brugger and Papenfuse, *Maryland: A New Guide*, 232.

65. "Historic Shore: Fassitt House," Unattributed newspaper article dated October 16, 1975, vertical file, Salisbury, MD; Forman, *Early Manor and Plantation Houses*, 144; Swann, *Colonial & Historical Houses of Maryland*, 198.

66. "Fort Nonsense," *The Sun*, October 29, 1983; "What's This Classified Fort Nonsense," *Washington Post*, May 18, 1985; Maryland Historical Trust, Historic Sites Inventory No.: AA-80, location: David W. Taylor, NSRDC, Annapolis Laboratory, Church Road, Anne Arundel County. An 1814 map entitled "Rough Plan of The Defenses of The Harbour of Annapolis in Maryland, taken from a pencil sketch made [by or for] Brigadier General Winder, Augt. 3d, 1816, by Wm Tatham Togpr. Engineer (Library of Congress) states "Fort Madison commanded by hill in its rear."

67. "Says Gen. Lingan Was Not Killed," *Baltimore American*, March 11, 1905; *Norfolk Gazette*, August 12, 1812.

68. "Find Two Skeletons," *The Sun*, March 9, 1905.

69. Maryland General Assembly, *Report of the Committee of Grievances*. The three indications of possible doubt are: the deposition of William Gwyen, who stated, "From his appearance, I believed him to be General Lingan," (page 28); the deposition of David R. Geddes, who stated, "Wednesday morning the 29th I there saw Mumma. I believe it to have been him holding in his hand the sheet that covered General Lingan, who was laying dead on the floor. He said to me, Look at the damn'd old Tory General! His language was shocking to the feeling of humanity," (page 53); and the deposition of Isaac Dickson, who claimed that he "could not tell if it was Lingan or Lee," (page 86).

70. *Salem Gazette*, October 5, 1784; *Providence Gazette*, February 16, 1782.

71. *New York Spectator*, July 30, 1806.

72. Extract from a Fast Day sermon by F.S.F. Gardiner of Boston as printed in the *Boston Courier*, April 21, 1808.

73. "Jean Lafitte: History and Mystery," Jean Lafitte National Historical Park and Preserve.

74. *The Sun*, October 12, 1880.

75. Scharf, *History of Baltimore City and County*, 112.

76. *Carlisle Gazette*, October 27, 1813.

77. *Niles' Weekly Register*, 1811, vol. 7, 112. Reprinted article from the *New Bedford Mercury*.

78. "Very Valuable Property," *Baltimore Patriot*, June 4, 1831.

79. "Baltimore's Proud Day," *The Sun*, September 12, 1888.

80. Quote from Louisa Sterett printed in *The Sun*, September 12, 1888; Lord, *The Dawn's Early Light*, 290. Lord provides a different version: "Captains Brown, Wilcox and McNamara of the 53rd Regiment, Royal Marines, have received everything they could desire at this house, notwithstanding it was received at the hands of the butler and in the absence of the colonel"; Lydia Hollingsworth to Ruth H., September 30, 1814; Stump, "Joseph Sterett," *Sunday Sun*, October 21, 1949. Surrey, though altered and damaged by a 1920s fire, still stands at 4901 Wilbur Avenue near Federal Street overlooking the Philadelphia Road. Some say the present house actually dates from after the War of 1812; "Mrs. Louisa Sterett Hollins," *The Sun*, October 7, 1889.

81. "Ode to a Rooster," *Baltimore Patriot and Evening Advertiser*, November 24, 1814; "The Bird of War," *Niles' Weekly Register*, supplement to Volume 7, 1815, 192.

82. "The Bird of War," *Niles' Weekly Register*, supplement to Volume 7, 1815, 192.

83. Scharf, *The Chronicles of Baltimore*, 353; *New York Times*, September 11, 1911.

84. "Offers Proof That Cock Did Crow at Ft. McHenry," *Evening Sun*, September 15, 1932.

85. Young, *The Citizen Soldiers*, 65.

86. Naval History and Heritage, "Saratoga," *Dictionary of American Naval Fighting Ships*.

87. Roger Brooke Taney (1777–1864), a former law partner of Key in Georgetown, became the chief justice of the U.S. Supreme Court from 1836 to 1864.

88. Filby and Howard, *Star-Spangled Books*, 51–55. This volume, written by the director of the Maryland Historical Society and a consultant, are considered by many as the authoritative reference on Key, Nicholson and Skinner's whereabouts and events surrounding the printing of Key's lyrics.

89. "Incidents of the War of the 1812," *Maryland Historical Magazine*, 340–47; *Baltimore Patriot*, May 23, 1849.

90. Letter from Honorable Chief Justice Taney in *Poems of the Late Francis S. Key*, 12–28.

91. Svejda, *History of The Star-Spangled Banner*, 76–83.

92. Captain Joseph H. Nicholson to Brigadier General William Winder, September 16.

93. Captain Joseph H. Nicholson to Secretary of War John Armstrong, September 18, 1814.

94. Abraham Lincoln Papers.

95. "The Star-Spangled Banner," *American Historical Record*, 721-34.

96. Elizabeth P. Howard to [unknown], March 27, [no year given but 1800s].
In 1825,
Elizabeth married Charles Howard, the son of Revolutionary War John
Edgar Howard.

97. The *President* packet operated as early as 1794 between Norfolk and
Baltimore and was described by a passenger as "a schooner, an excellent
sailer, well built with attractive passenger cabins." See Footner's *Tidewater
Triumph*, 54-55.

98. Logbook of HM frigate *Surprise*, September 7, 1814.

99. Sisco, "The Nancy Prince Collection."

100. Captain Joseph H. Nicholson to Secretary of Navy William Jones,
August 28, 1814.

101. Captain Joseph H. Nicholson to Secretary of State James Monroe,
September 1, 1814; Nicholson to Mrs. Albert Gallatin, September 4,
1814.

102. Ibid. See also Sheads, "Joseph Hopper Nicholson," 146.

103. Major General Samuel Smith to Major George Armistead, November
6, 1815.

104. Ibid.; Armistead to Smith, November 6, 1815; Samuel Smith to George
Harryman, December 8, 1815. Harryman was brigade quartermaster for
the 11th Brigade under General Tobias Stansbury during the Battle for
Baltimore.

105. "Obituary," *The Sun*, June 28, 1878.

106. Ibid.

107. "Part of the Star-Spangled Banner Now Walker Heirloom," *The Sun*,
November 8, 1973.

108. "A Precious Remnant," *The Sun*, December 18, 1896.

109. "History Makers Great in Death," *The Sun*, September 28, 1903.

110. "A Precious Remnant," *The Sun*, December 18, 1896.

111. Ibid.

112. "The Soldiers Return," *The Sun*, June 3, 1842.

113. "Relic Buried with Her," *The Sun*, January 18, 1902; "Obituary,"
The Sun, January 17, 1902; "History Makers Great in Death," *The Sun*,
September 28, 1903.

114. "Part of the Star-Spangled Banner now Walker Heirloom," *The Sun*,
November 8, 1973.

115. "Fishing for Cannon," *The Sun*, May 2, 1873.

116. "Dr. Jacob Houck and the Battle of North Point," *The Sun*, September 16, 1907.

117. Browne, "Battle of North Point"; *The Sun*, September 8, 1907. The article also was published in the *Book of the Royal Blue*, a 1907 publication of the Baltimore and Ohio Railroad; General George R. Willis, the great nephew of Eleanor, gave a lecture entitled "Sidelights on the Character of Gen. Robert Ross" before the Maryland Historical Society on November 9, 1914.

118. Bennett, *Never Prod A Hornet*, 36–37, 39.

119. "Foulke Farmhouse," National Register of Historic Places Inventory, No. RA-147.

120. "Attack upon Baltimore," *Niles' Weekly Register*, September 24, 1814, 23–25.

121. Marine, *The British Invasion of Maryland*, 150, footnote 5. Marine gives his source as "Oration of H. Clay Dallam, 1878." Judge Henry Clay Dallam (1828–87), a law graduate of the University of Maryland, gave the oration on September 13, 1878, at Hall's Springs, Baltimore; "Old Defenders Day," *The Sun*, September 13, 1887.

122. Hawkins, *Life of John W. Hawkins*.

123. Examples include Lord's *The Dawn's Early Light* (261–262) and George's *Terror on the Chesapeake* (137).

124. Hickey, *Don't Give Up The Ship!*, 85.

125. Much of this information was provided by Larry Leone to Ralph Eshelman during a tour of the area.

126. Browne, "Battle of North Point"; *The Sun*, September 8, 1907.

127. "A Relic Gone" *The Sun*, March 22, 1844.

128. Ibid.

129. "A Log of the Proceedings of HM Ship Royal Oak, Joseph Pearce, Esq.," ADM 51/2760, Captain's Log, HMS Royal Oak, Public Records Office, The National Archives, London England.

130. *Daily National Intelligencer*, May 21, 1813.

131. *Alexandria Gazette*, October 29, 1814.

132. "Communicated," *American and Commercial Daily Advertiser*, November 4, 1815.

133. See also "General Ross," *Federal Gazette*, October 27, 1815; "Communication," *American and Commercial Daily Advertiser*, November 4, 1815; John McCavitt brought the *American Beacon* article to the attention of the authors.

134. "To the Editors of the American," *American and Commercial Daily Advertiser*, November 6, 1815.

135. "General Benjamin Chew Howard," *National Intelligencer*, October 1, 1839.

136. Jenkins, "The Shots That Saved Baltimore," 364.

137. *Baltimore Patriot*, August 12, 1813.

138. Hickey, *Don't Give Up the Ship!*, 87, footnote 102; "From a Gentleman," *American Watchman*, September 28, 1814. The possibility of canister shot is based on word from a gentleman in Fells Point who supposedly heard it from Colonel John S. Skinner, who had accompanied Francis Scott Key onboard the American flag of truce cartel anchored among the British fleet. No other sources substantiate this questionable claim.

139. Bennett, *Never Prod a Hornet*, 52–53.

140. Browne, "Battle of North Point." On the 1814 Winder map, an unnamed house stands along Schoolhouse Cove at Back River a mile from where the Aquila Randall Monument stands today. That may be the Stansbury House.

141. Trotten House vertical file, Dundalk Patapsco Neck Historical Society, Dundalk, Maryland.

142. "Battleground House," *Mercury Evening News*, September 19, 1911.

143. "Fought at North Point," *The Sun*, July 18, 1905; "Died," *American Mercury*, September 13, 1825; "Died," *The Sun*, May 10, 1859; *Hagerstown Gazette*, December 17, 1811.

144. *The Miscellaneous Documents of the Senate*, 3–5.

145. "Fought at North Point," *The Sun*, July 18, 1905: Obituary, Nathaniel F. Williams, *The Sun*, December 26, 1864; *American Mercury*, September 13, 1825. Caroline was the only daughter of Commodore Joshua Barney. She married Nathaniel Williams on October 14, 1809, and died on August 18, 1825.

146. Browne, "Battle of North Point."

147. Indenture of September 9, 1771, Provincial Court Land Records, 1770-1774, Maryland State Archives, Annapolis, MD. "Bread and Cheese Creek," *Provincial Court Land Records, 1770-1774, Maryland State Archives*, Accessed 2010-12-28. Robert G. Breen, "Lazy, Defiant Bread And Cheese Creek Found," *The Sun* (Baltimore), September 5, 1960. Interestingly the creek is not found in Hamill Kenny's *The Place Names of Maryland: Their Origin and Meaning* (Baltimore: The Maryland Historical Society, 1988).

148. Heffernan, "History of 'Abington Manor.'"

149. Ibid.

150. Jones, "Woodlawn."

151. Sister Mary Xavier, *Grandma's Stories*. Xavier's account is repeated in Klapthor's "Southern Maryland During The War of 1812," 1–5. Her

full name is given as Sister Mary Xavier Queen in her obituary in the December 6, 1906 issue of *The Sun.*

152. Browning, *Forty-Four Years*, 166–67.

153. Paulding, *The Lay of the Scottish Fiddle.*

154. Duyckinck, *Cyclopedia of American Literature.*

155. *Niles' Weekly Register*, May 15, 1813.

156. Gleig, *Campaigns of the British Army*, 56.

157. *Baltimore Whig*, September 2, 1813.

158. *American and Commercial Daily Advertiser*, August 31, 1813.

159. Captain Robert Barrie to Admiral John B. Warren, November 14, 1814. Reprinted in *The Naval War of 1812*, vol. 2, edited by William S. Dudley, 395–96.

160. Heitman, *Historical Register and Dictionary*, I:716; Fredriksen, *The United States Army in the War of 1812*, 179.

161. Youmans, "Eight Days In May."

162. Ibid.

163. See http://en.wikipedia.org/wiki/War_hawk.

164. *Maryland Republican*, July 15, 1809. John W. Butler, editor of the *Maryland Republican*, may have been the person who wrote this earliest known definition of the phrase, though its usage dates from at least 1793, when the word "War Hawks" was first known to have been used in an American newspaper.

165. *Eastern Herald*, June 1, 1793.

166. *Eastern Shore Republican Star and General Advertiser*, March 8, 1803.

167. Eshelman and Kummerow, *In Full Glory Reflected*, 55.

168. Lieutenant Colonel Thomas M. Bayly to Governor James Barbour, May 31, 1814. Reprinted in *United States Gazette*, July 2, 1814; Virginia State Records, Governor's Office (RG3), Executive Papers, Governor James Barbour, 1812–1814; Reprinted in Whitelaw's *Virginia's Eastern Shore*, 816.

169. June 25, 1814, National Library of Scotland, Alexander F.I. Cochrane Papers, MS 2333, fols. 123–32.

170. The full title of this book is *The Parson of the Islands: A Biography of the Rev. Joshua Thomas; Embracing Sketches of His Contemporaries, and Remarkable Camp Meeting Scenes, Revival Incidents, and Reminiscences of the Introduction of Methodism on the Islands of the Chesapeake, and the Eastern Shores of Maryland and Virginia.*

171. All quotes said to be by Reverend Joshua Thomas are originally from the Reverend Levin M. Prettyman manuscript (circa 1840), an early attempt to publish a biography of Thomas while he was still living.

Presumably, Prettyman interviewed Thomas, incorporating his quotes into his manuscript, which was never completed but was heavily used by Reverend Wallace in his 1861 biography.

172. "City's Peril Recalled," *The Sun*, August 28, 1905; "Parson of the Isles" *The Sun*, October 21, 1906.
173. Wallace, *Parson of the Islands*, 148.
174. *Virginia Argus*, September 17, 1812.
175. *Virginia Argus*, October 12, 1812.
176. *Richmond Enquirer*, November 20, 1812; *Niles' Weekly Register*, November 28, 1812
177. *Virginia Patriot*, December 8, 1812, and September 21, 1813.
178. Lorrain, *The Helm, the Sword and the Cross*, 103.
179. *Virginia Patriot*, December 8, 1812.
180. *Virginia Patriot*, September 21, 1813.
181. Ryan and Wallace Jr., "Duty and Honor."
182. Alexandria Mayor Charles Simms to his wife Nancy Simms, September 3, 1814.
183. Captain Charles Napier, commander of HM frigate *Eurylaus*, as quoted in Muller's "Fabulous Potomac Passage," 89.
184. Alexandria Mayor Charles Simms to his wife Nancy Simms, September 3, 1814.
185. *Niles' Weekly Register*, August 21, 1813. Boyle lived at Pugh Town or Pughtown, now known as Gainesboro, Frederick County, Virginia.
186. Eshelman and Kummerow, *In Full Glory Reflected*, 27.
187. *Baltimore Patriot*, July 23, 1813.
188. Margaret Ann Bonyer to Sally Wyatt Bibb, June 30, 1813. Quote taken from Hampton History Museum exhibit with source given as Dorothy Rouse-Bottom.
189. Colonel Sir Thomas Sidney Beckwith to Adm. Sir John Borlace Warren, July 5, 1813. Reprinted in *The Naval War of 1812*, vol. 2, 364–65.
190. *Daily National Intelligencer*, July 2, 1813.
191. *Baltimore Patriot*, July 23, 1813.
192. Lossing, *Pictorial Field-Book*, 687, footnote 2.
193. "A 'Jug Wasps' Nest," *The Sun*, January 11, 1898.
194. Browne, "Battle of North Point."
195. "New York Publication Reprints Article from Calvert Independent," *Calvert Independent*, 1961. The article refers to a 1941 article but gives no date.
196. Clausen, *Insect Fact and Folklore*, 118–21.
197. Bennett, *Never Prod a Hornet*, 40–41.

198. "The Swampoodle Book, 47–48.

199. "Anecdote of the War of 1812," *Alexandria Gazette*, March 24, 1847.

200. Scott, *Recollections of a Naval Life*, vol. 3, 65.

201. *American Watchman and Delaware Republican*, February 24, 1813.

202. *Daily National Intelligencer*, August 2, 1813.

203. Clement Dorsey to Brigadier General Philip Stuart, *Maryland Gazette and Political Intelligencer*, June 23, 1814. Reprinted from *Daily National Intelligencer*, June 20, 1814.

204. There is no documentation to support this Mount Arundel story. See also George's *Terror on the Chesapeake* (pages 173–74) for his claim that incidents of poisoning may have been British paranoia.

205. Scott, *Recollections of a Naval Life*, vol. 3, 243–44.

206. *Niles' Weekly Register*, August 6, 1814.

207. Rear Admiral George Cockburn to Vice Admiral Alexander Cochrane, July 21, 1814. Reprinted in *The Naval War of 1812*, vol. 3, 165.

208. Lieutenant Colonel Richard E. Parker, 11th [actually 35th] Virginia Regiment to Adjutant General of Virginia, Wicomico Church, VA, July 24, 1814, *Baltimore Patriot*, August 5, 1814.

209. *Niles' Weekly Register*, August 6, 1814.

210. Lieutenant Christopher Claxton to Captain Thomas Hardy, September 16, 1814. George's *Terror on the Chesapeake* reprints this account (174).

211. Browne, "Battle of North Point."

212. Bennett, *Never Prod a Hornet*, 32–33.

213. Jefferson, *Notes on the State of Virginia*, 31–32.

214. "Bridge Burned by the British," *Washington Post*, March 9, 1902.

215. "The Goths at Washington," *Niles' Weekly Register*, December 31, 1814.

216. Commodore Thomas Tingey to Secretary of the Navy William Jones, November 9, 1814. Reprinted in *The Naval War of 1812*, vol. 3, 320–21.

217. Secretary of the Navy William Jones to Congressman Richard M. Johnson, October 3, 1814. reprinted in *The Naval War of 1812*, vol. 3, 311–18.

218. Sala, *My Diary*, 104–06.

219. Ibid.

220. Haley, *Philip's Washington Described*.

221. "Capture of Washington by the British in 1814," *Daily Iowa State Register*, August 25, 1869; "Historic Washington," *Evening Star*, December 24, 1880.

222. There are several places where Mrs. Madison's papers can be viewed, including http://rotunda.upress.virginia.edu/dmde.

223. David Mattern, an editor of James Madison's papers, states that the original letter does not exist. Historians use a transcript or extract of the letter that Dolley Madison copied from *The National Portrait Gallery of Distinguished Americans*, published over twenty years after the event. At some point, Mrs. Madison copied it out of the book in her own handwriting. This transcription is the only record of the letter in her handwriting. While Mrs. Madison regularly corresponded with friends and family, this particular letter differs in its tone and formality. She provides details that would seem unnecessary if she were simply writing to her sister.

224. Letter from Dolley Madison to Robert G.L. De Peyster. Reprinted in Mattern and Shulman, eds., *The Selected Letters of Dolley Payne Madison*, 387.

225. Burke, "Witness to History."

226. "The Capture of Washington," *New York Commercial Advertiser*, May 13, 1847.

227. Ibid.

228. Other newspapers of the time suggest severe storms were also taking place from New York to South Carolina. *Otsego Herald* (NY), August 25, 1814; *Poulson's American Daily Advertiser* (PA), August 24, 1814.

229. Conner, *Birthstone of the White House and Capitol*, 107, 151.

230. Hickey, *Don't Give Up the Ship*, 81. Hickey provides two instances of the term "White House" being used prior to its burning in 1814. See also Seale, *The White House*, 35; Unger, *The Last Founding Father*, 277.

231. Barney, *A Biographical Memoir*, 267.

232. Commodore Joshua Barney to Secretary of Navy William Jones, August 29, 1814.

233. Barney, *A Biographical Memoir*, 266–70. William Bedford Barney, born 1780, died on November 18, 1838; *The Sun*, November 20, 1838; Footner, *Sailor of Fortune*, 303–04.

234. "D.A.R. Gets Barney Relics," *The Sun*, June 27, 1919.

234. *Washington Herald*, June 25, 1911.

235. "A Fence of Gun Barrels," *Baltimore American*, October 13, 1911; "Affairs in Georgetown," *Evening Star*, December 12, 1866; Daw, *A Stranger's Guide Book*, 27; Ferrall "Commencement Exercises."

Glossary

NOTE: Words in this glossary are marked in the text by an asterisk (*). Many words have more than one meaning, and the definitions of words change over time. This glossary defines words as used in context during the War of 1812.

bollard: A short vertical post originally used on a ship or a dock, principally for mooring watercraft.

bombardment: To assault with bombs shot from mortars, such as during the bombardment of Fort McHenry.

brevette: A commission promoting a military officer in rank without an increase in pay.

brig: Type of sailing vessel with two square-rigged masts considered fast and maneuverable and used as both naval warships and merchant vessels.

Britannia metal: A pewter-type alloy favored for its silvery appearance and smooth surface.

brogan: A large log canoe made of seven or more logs fastened together and hollowed out. A brogan was not only larger than a log canoe* but also had a partial deck over the hull, unlike the open canoe.

canister shot: Anti-personnel scattershot for cannon consisting of musket balls packed into a sheet-metal cylinder closed at each end by a tight-fitting iron disc held in place by crimped tabs. Chain links, scraps of metal, shards of glass, rocks, etc. were also sometimes used. On firing, the balls spread out from the muzzle at high velocity, giving an effect similar to that of a shotgun but scaled up to cannon size.

cannonade: To assault with heavy cannon fire. Bombardment is often confused with cannonading.

carronade: A type of short, lightweight cannon capable of firing a relatively heavy caliber shot, typically carried on the upper deck of a ship for short-range use. Named after the Carron Ironworks in Scotland, where it was first made in the 1780s.

cartel ship: Employed on humanitarian voyages, in particular, to carry prisoners for exchange or negotiate terms of exchange. While serving as a cartel, a ship was not subject to capture.

Chesapeake: Approximately two hundred miles long from the Susquehanna River in the north to the Atlantic Ocean in the south, the Chesapeake Bay is the largest estuary in the United States and is surrounded by Maryland and Virginia with a shoreline of over eleven thousand miles.

Congreve Rocket: Self-propelled projectile invented by William Congreve, consisting of a cylindrical sheet-iron chamber filled with black powder, capped with a warhead and strapped to a long wooden staff to help provide stability during flight. Propulsion gases were exhausted through a nozzle in the rear. One could also ignite a fuse to detonate an explosive warhead that, if used, could contain musket balls or combustible materials. Available in several sizes with ranges up to two miles. Launched from ships or on land from portable copper tubes or wooden lattices often supported by a tripod.

corvette: A small, maneuverable, lightly armed warship. Smaller than a frigate and used mostly for coastal patrol and supporting large fleets.

dragoon: Mounted infantry who were trained in horse riding as well as infantry fighting skills. Over time, dragoons evolved into conventional light cavalry units. The name is possibly derived from a type of firearm called a dragon carried by dragoons of the French Army.

earthwork: Fortifications constructed from soil that, when made thick enough, could provide adequate protection from weapons. Because soil was usually readily available in huge quantities, it was often used to construct defenses such as gun emplacements, trenches and bastions.

frigate: A vessel of war, three-masted, fully rigged, in size between a corvette and a ship of the line. Frigates in the Chesapeake had a full-length gun deck that typically carried thirty-six or thirty-eight long guns in the Royal Navy and thirty-eight or forty-four guns in the U.S. Navy. When carronades were introduced, the thirty-eight-gun class frigates carried forty-four or more large-caliber guns, while the forty-four-gun class frigate carried fifty-six or more.

grapeshot: Instead of a single solid shot (cannonball), grapeshot consisted of nine metal balls packed in tiers of three around a center post on a circular iron tray called a stool and contained by a cinched canvas bag or netting resembling a cluster of grapes (hence the name). Canister shot was larger and had a greater range and penetration than grapeshot. It was often used to disable a ship's sails and rigging.

gun battery: A unit of guns, mortars or rockets grouped together to better facilitate battlefield command and control.

gunboat: A small vessel of shallow draft carrying one or more cannons of large caliber; or any small vessels fitted for carrying cannon.

impressment: The act of taking men into a navy by force and without notice.

log canoe: A type of small craft developed in the Chesapeake Bay region, made from two, three or five logs fastened together and hollowed out. The sides were heightened by adding wooden planks. These vessels were the principal traditional fishing boats of the bay. Reverend Thomas's log craft was technically a brogan.*

militia: A military force composed of ordinary citizens to provide defense, emergency law enforcement or paramilitary service in times of emergency. One who serves in the militia is a militiaman.

Orders in Council: A type of legislation in the United Kingdom where legislation is formally made in the name of the ruling monarch.

packet vessel: Small boats designed for domestic mail, passenger and freight transportation.

Peninsula War: A military conflict between France and the allied powers of Spain, the United Kingdom and Portugal for control of the Iberian Peninsula during the Napoleonic Wars.

pounder: Cannons are identified by the weight of the cannonball they fire. Thus, a six-pounder cannon fires a six-pound ball.

ropewalk: A long, straight, narrow lane, covered pathway or shed where long strands of material were laid before being twisted into rope.

row galley: An armed watercraft that used oars rather than sail as a means of propulsion

scow: A flat-bottomed boat with a blunt bow, often used to haul freight.

Sea Fencibles: Naval militia, generally mariners by trade, equipped and organized under the authority of the U.S. War Department.

ship of the line: A type of naval warship constructed from the seventeenth through the mid-nineteenth centuries to take part in the naval tactic known as line of battle, in which two columns of opposing warships would maneuver to bring the greatest weight broadside guns to bear. Since these engagements were almost invariably won by the heaviest ships carrying the most powerful guns, the natural progression was to build sailing vessels that were the largest and most powerful of their time. Ships of the line normally carried 74 guns, but the number could vary from 60 to 120.

sloop: A sailing vessel with a single mast and a fore-and-aft rig.

sloop of war: A warship smaller than a frigate,* with a single-gun deck that carried up to eighteen guns.

tender: A boat used to service a ship, generally for transporting people and/or supplies to and from shore or another ship.

vandalic: Pertaining to vandalism.

wad: A plug of hay, straw, cloth or paper made up into a tight ball and placed down the gun barrel after the powder and rammed tight to keep the powder compacted. A wad also retains the powder charge in the muzzle while loading a gun or cannon.

waterman: Person who makes their living by oystering, clamming, fishing, etc. on the Chesapeake Bay.

Bibliography

Alexandria Gazette (VA). "Anecdote of the War of 1812." March 24, 1847.

———. October 29, 1814.

American and Commercial Daily Advertiser (Baltimore). "Battle of the Ice Mound." February 22, 1815.

———. "Communication." November 4, 1815.

———. "To the Editors of the American." November 6, 1815.

———. August 31, 1813.

———. August 12, 1814.

American Watchman (DE). "From a Gentleman." September 28, 1814.

American Watchman and Delaware Republican. February 24, 1813.

Arnett, Earl, Robert J. Brugger, and Edward C. Papenfuse. *Maryland: A New Guide to the Old Line State.* Baltimore: The Johns Hopkins University Press, 1999.

Baltimore American. "A Fence of Gun Barrels." October 13, 1911.

————. "St. Michaels Defense." September 6, 1897.

————. "Says Gen. Lingan Was Not Killed: Supposed Victim of Riot of 1812 Escaped to Canada, Claims Mr. J.W. Smith." March 11, 1905.

————. April 17, 22, 1890.

Baltimore Patriot. "Parker, Lieutenant Colonel Richard E. to Adjutant General Moses Green of Virginia." July 24, 1814 and August 5, 1814.

————. "Very Valuable Property." June 4, 1831.

————. August 12, 1813.

————. July 23, 1813.

————. May 23, 1849.

————. September 2, 1813.

————. September 5, 1814.

Baltimore Patriot and Evening Advertiser. "Ode to a Rooster." November 24, 1814.

Barden, Thomas E., ed. *Virginia Folk Legends*. Charlottesville: University Press of Virginia, 1991.

Barney, Mary. *A Biographical Memoir of the Late Commodore Joshua Barney*. Boston: Gray and Bowen, 1832.

Barrett, C.R.B. *The 85ʰ King's Light Infantry*. London: Spottiswoode & Co., Ltd., 1913.

Bennett, Esther Wingert. *Never Prod a Hornet: A Story About the War of 1812*. Baltimore: H.G. Roebuck & Son, Inc., 1966.

Beynon, First Lieutenant Benjamin G. "A Journal Kept Aboard HMS *Menelaus* in the Chesapeake Bay, 1813–1815." Western Reserve Historical Society, Cleveland, OH. MS. 1236, cabinet 40, drawer 8.

Boston Courier. "Extract from a Fast Day Sermon by F.S.F. Gardiner of Boston." April 21, 1808.

Breen, Robert G. "Lazy, Defiant Bread and Cheese Creek Found." *The Sun,* September 5, 1960.

Browne, Reverend Lewis B. "Battle of North Point in Legend and Tradition." *The Sun,* September 8, 1907.

———. "The Battle of North Point in Legend and Tradition: How the British Marched Upon Baltimore and then Marched Back Again." *Baltimore and Ohio Railroad Magazine* 10, August 1907.

Browning, Meshach. *Forty-Four Years of the Life of a Hunter; Being Reminiscences of Meshach Browning, a Maryland Hunter; Roughly Written Down by Himself, Revised and illustrated by E. Stabler.* Reprint. Winston-Salem, NC: Winston Printing Company, 1942.

Burke, Kathleen. "Witness to History: The First Memoir by a White House Slave Recreates the Events of August 23, 1814." *Smithsonian Magazine,* March 2010.

Calvert Independent (MD). "New York Publication Reprints Article from Calvert Independent." 1961.

Caperton, Helena Lefroy. *Legends of Virginia.* Whitefish, MT: Kessinger Publishing, 2010.

Carey, George G. *Maryland Folklore and Folklife.* Cambridge, MD: Tidewaters Publishers, 1970.

Carlisle Gazette (PA). October 27, 1813.

Carmack, Sharon DeBartolo. *Your Guide to Cemetery Research.* Cincinnati: Betterway Books, 2002.

Chandlee Forman. *Early Manor and Plantation Houses of Maryland.* Baltimore: Bodine & Associates, Inc., 1982.

Clausen, Lucy Wilhelmine. *Insect Fact and Folklore.* New York: Macmillan Company, 1954.

Conner, Jane Hollenbeck. *Birthstone of the White House and Capitol.* Virginia Beach, VA: Donning Company Publishers, 2005.

Daily Iowa State Register. "Capture of Washington by the British in 1814," August 25, 1869.

Daw, Reuben. *The Washington and Georgetown Directory: A Stranger's Guide Book for Washington.* Washington, D.C.: Kirkwood and McGill, 1853.

Dawson, James. "Did St. Michaels Really Fool the British in the War of 1812?" *Tidewater Times,* August 2012.

———. "Gentleman George, Defender of Easton in the War of 1812." *Tidewater Times,* December 2012.

Dobbin, Muriel. "A Shot that Named a Town." *The Sun,* July 30, 1961.

Duyckinck, George, and Edward Duyckinck. *Cyclopedia of American Literature.* New York: Charles Scribner's Sons, 1856.

Eastern Herald (ME). June 1, 1793.

Eastern Shore Republican Star and General Advertiser (MD). March 8, 1803.

Easton Gazette (MD). "Death of a Veteran." March 7, 1848.

———. "Death of the Royal Oak." July 31, 1858.

———. "Lines, Suggested by Reading an Account of the Death of the Royal Oak Near Easton, Md." August 14, 1858.

Easton Star (MD). "Fort Stokes, Its History." February 19, 1861.

———. "Great Union Victory at Cow Landing." January 19, 1862.

Eshelman, Ralph. *A Travel Guide to the War of 1812 in the Chesapeake: Eighteen Tours in Maryland, Virginia, and the District of Columbia.* Baltimore: The Johns Hopkins University Press, 2011.

Eshelman, Ralph, and Burton Kummerow. *In Full Glory Reflected: Discovering the War of 1812 in the Chesapeake.* Baltimore: Maryland Historical Society Press and Maryland Historical Trust Press, 2012.

Eshelman, Ralph, Scott Sheads and Donald Hickey. *The War of 1812 in the Chesapeake: A Reference Guide to Historic Sites In Maryland, Virginia, and the District of Columbia.* Baltimore: The Johns Hopkins University Press, 2010.

Evening Star (Washington, D.C.). "Affairs in Georgetown." December 12, 1866.

————. "Historic Washington." December 24, 1880.

Federal Gazette (Baltimore). "General Ross." October 27, 1815.

————. September 7, 1814.

Federal Republican (Baltimore). "Jacob Gibson." May 5, 1813.

Federal Writer's Project. *Maryland: A Guide to the Old Line State.* New York: Oxford University Press, 1940.

Ferrall, John A. "Commencement Exercises—and Other Things." *The Volta Review,* 21, no. 2 (December 1919).

Filby, P.W., and Edward G. Howard. *Star-Spangled Books: Books, Sheet Music, Newspapers, Manuscripts, and Persons Associated with "The Star-Spangled Banner."* Baltimore: Maryland Historical Society, 1972.

Flowers, Thomas A., ed. *Dorchester Tercentenary Bay Country Festival, 1669–1969.* Cambridge, MD: Dorchester County Commissioners, 1969.

Footner, Geoffrey. *Tidewater Triumph: The Development and Worldwide Success of the Chesapeake Bay Pilot Schooner.* Annapolis, MD: Naval Institute Press, 1998.

Footner, Hulbert. *Sailor of Fortune: The Life and Adventures of Joshua Barney*. New York: Harper & Brothers, 1940.

Ford, Fred. "The Battle of St. Paul's Church Yard." *Kent County News* (MD), June 15, 1977.

Fredriksen, John C. *The United States Army in the War of 1812: Concise Biographies of Commanders and Operational Histories of Regiments with Bibliographies of Published and Primary Resources*. Jefferson, NC: McFarland & Company, Inc., 2009.

Genealogy.com. Discussion under William Cardiff Killman. http://genforum.genealogy.com/killman/messages/113.html.

George, Christopher. *Terror on the Chesapeake: The War of 1812 on the Bay*. Shippensburg, PA: White Mane Books, 2000.

Ghosts of DC. "Georgetown's Gun Barrel Fence." http://ghostsofdc.org/2012/09/24/georgetown-gun-barrel-fence/

Gleig, George Robert. *The Campaigns of the British Army at Washington and New Orleans*. Reprint of 1847 edition. Lanham, MD: Roman and Littlefield, 1972.

Graves, Donald E. "Why the White House Was Burned: An Investigation into the British Destruction of Public Buildings at Washington in August 1814." *The Journal of Military History* 76 (October 2012): 1095–1127.

Hagerstown Gazette (MD). December 17, 1811.

Haley, William D. *Philip's Washington Described: A Complete View of the American Capitol and the District of Columbia*. New York: Rudd & Carleton, 1861.

Hanks, Douglas, Jr. *Tales of Sharp's Island*. Easton, MD: Economy Printing, 1971.

Hawkins, Reverend William George. *Life of John W. Hawkins, Compiled by His Son*. Boston, 1859.

Healey, David. *1812: Rediscovering Chesapeake Bay's Forgotten War*. Rock Hill, SC: Bella Rosa Books, 2005.

Heffernan, B.J. "History of 'Abington Manor.'" Unpublished, undated three-page typed manuscript. Calvert County Historic District Commission, Prince Frederick, Maryland.

Heitman, Francis B. *Historical Register and Dictionary of the United States Army.* Washington, DC: Government Printing Office, 1903.

Hemstock, Kevin, "Quiet Monument Belied as Explosive Past," *Tales of Kent County, Volume Two*, 2006.

Hickey, Donald R. *Don't Give Up the Ship!: Myths of the War of 1812.* Urbana: University of Illinois Press, 2006.

"Historic Shore: Fassitt House." Unidentified newspaper article dated October 16, 1975. Vertical file. Edward H. Nabb Research Center for Delmarva History and Culture, Salisbury University, Salisbury, Maryland.

"Howard, Elizabeth P. to [unknown], March 27 [no year given but 1800s]." Fort McHenry Library, Baltimore, Maryland.

"Incidents of the War of the 1812." Reprint of John Stuart Skinner letter in *Baltimore Patriot*, May 23, 1849. *Maryland Historical Magazine* 32, no. 4. (December 1937): 340–47.

Ingraham, Prentiss. *Land of Legendary Lore: Sketches of Romance and Reality on the Eastern Shore of the Chesapeake.* Easton, MD: The Gazette Publishing House, 1898.

Jefferson, Thomas. *Notes on the State of Virginia.* Philadelphia: Prichard and Hall, 1788.

Jenkins, B. Wheeler. "The Shots That Saved Baltimore." *Maryland Historical Magazine* 77, no. 4 (Winter 1982): 362–64.

Jones, Elias. *Keene Family History and Genealogy.* Madison, WI: Kohn and Pollock, Inc, 1923.

Jones, Mrs. Ray. "Woodlawn." Unpublished, two-page typed manuscript dated 1939. Noted as copied by Mrs. Carrow Prout in 1954. Calvert County Historic District Commission, Prince Frederick, Maryland.

Kessler, Glenn. "The Fact Checker." *Washington Post*, December 16, 2012.

Klapthor, Margaret Brown. "Southern Maryland During the War of 1812." *The Record* (Historical Society of Charles County), April 1965.

Library of Congress. *Abraham Lincoln Papers at the Library of Congress.* http://memory.loc.gov/ammem/alhtml/malhome.html.

Lord, Walter. *The Dawn's Early Light.* New York: W.W. Norton & Co., 1972.

Lorrain, Alfred M. *The Helm, the Sword and the Cross: A Life Narrative.* Cincinnati, 1862.

Lossing, Benson J. *The Pictorial Field-Book of the War of 1812.* New York: Harper Bros., 1868.

Madison, Dolley. Letter to Robert G.L. De Peyster, February 11, 1848. Reprinted in David B. Mattern and Holly C. Shulman, eds. *The Selected Letters of Dolley Payne Madison.* Charlottesville: University of Virginia Press, 2003.

Marine, William M. *The British Invasion of Maryland, 1812–1815.* Reprint of 1914 edition. Hatboro, PA: Tradition Press, 1965.

Maryland Gazette and Political Intelligencer. Dorsey, Clement, Letter to Brigadier General Philip Stuart, June 23, 1814. Reprinted from *National Intelligencer,* June 20, 1814.

Maryland General Assembly. *Report of the Committee of Grievances and Courts of Justice of the House of Delegates of Maryland, on the Subject of the Recent Mobs and Riots in the City of Baltimore, Together with the Depositions Taken Before the Committee.* Annapolis, MD: Jonas Green, 1813.

Maryland Republican. July 15, 1809.

Mills, Charles A. *Treasure Legends of Virginia.* Alexandria, VA: Apple Cheeks Press, 1984.

The Miscellaneous Documents of the Senate of the United States for the First Session of the Thirty-fifth Congress, Volume 2. Washington, D.C.: William A. Harris, 1858.

Morning Mail (London). May 15, 1815.

Muller, Charles G. "Fabulous Potomac Passage." *United States Naval Institute Proceedings*, 90 (May 1964): 89.

National Intelligencer (Washington, D.C.). "Huzza for the Militia Chestertown, Maryland, Dated September 1." September 5, 1814.

———. July 2, 1813.

National Register of Historic Places. Foulke Farmhouse/Shaw House, Sparrows Point, Baltimore County, Maryland, National Register #BA-147.

Naval History and Heritage. "Saratoga," *Dictionary of American Fighting Ships*, http://www.history.navy.mil/danfs/s6/saratoga-ii.htm.

New York Commercial Advertiser. "The Capture of Washington." May 13, 1847.

New York Spectator. July 30, 1806.

New York Times. September 11, 1911.

Niles' Weekly Register. "The Attack Upon Baltimore." vol. 7, no. 2, September 24, 1814, 23–25.

———. "Bird of War." Supplement to vol. 7, 1815, 192.

———. "The Goths at Washington." December 31, 1814. Originally printed in the *London Statesman*.

———. Reed, Lieutenant Colonel Philip to Brigadier General Benjamin Chambers, September 3, 1814. vol. 7, 150.

———. August 21, 1813.

———. August 6, 1814.

———. May 21, 1813.

———. November 28, 1812.

Norfolk Gazette. August 12, 1812.

Otsego Herald (NY). August 25, 1814.

Paulding, James Kirke. *The Lay of the Scottish Fiddle: A Tale of Havre de Grace*. Philadelphia: Inskeep and Bradford, 1813.

Plummer, Norman H. "Another Look at the Battle of St. Michaels." *The Weather Gauge* (Spring 1995), 10–17.

Poulson's American Daily Advertiser (PA). August 24, 1814.

Providence Gazette. February 16, 1782.

Republican Star (Easton). May 31, 1814.

Republican Star (Somerset County, MD). "To the Editor of the Republican Star." May 23, 1814.

Richmond Enquirer. November 20, 1812.

Ryan, James H., and Lee A. Wallace Jr. "Duty and Honor: Petersburg's Contributions to the War of 1812." *Proceedings of the Historic Petersburg Foundation*, March 2004.

Rypka, Don. "From the Archives of St. Paul: Notes Surrounding September 1814." *St. Paul's Church Newsletter*, n.d.

Sala, George A. *My Diary in America in the Midst of War: Volume 2*. London: Tinsley Brothers, 1865.

Salem Gazette (MA). October 5, 1784.

Scharf, John Thomas. *The Chronicles of Baltimore: Being A Complete History of "Baltimore Town" and Baltimore City from the Earliest Period to the Present Time.* Baltimore: Turnbull Brothers, 1874.

———. *History of Baltimore City and County, Maryland.* Philadelphia, 1881.

Scott, James. *Recollections of a Naval Life* Vol. 3. London: Richard Bentley, 1834.

Seale, William. *The White House: The History of an American Idea.* Washington, D.C.: The American Institute of Architects Press, 1992.

Sewall, Thomas H. "The Battle of St. Michaels, 1813–1814." Howard I. Chapelle Library, Chesapeake Bay Maritime Museum, St. Michaels, Maryland.

Sheads, Scott S. "Joseph Hopper Nicholson: Citizen-Soldier of Maryland." *Maryland Historical Magazine,* 98, no. 2 (Summer 2003): 146.

Shulman, Holly C., ed. *The Dolley Madison Digital Edition.* http://rotunda. upress.virginia.edu/dmde/.

Sisco, Mark. "The Nancy Prince Collection of Folk Art and Native Americana." *Maine Antique Digest,* 2002.

———. "The Star-Spangled Banner." *American Historical Record* (January 1873): 721–34.

Smith, Doris. *Voices from the Cities of the Dead: A Cemetery Reference Guide to Understanding Terminologies, Gravestone Art, Monuments, Abbreviations, Symbols and Icons.* Daytona Beach, FL: Raven's Loch Publishing House, 2004.

Star Democrat (Easton, MD). "Thomas Norton." May 16, 2005.

Stewart, Robert G., "The Battle of the Ice Mound, February 7, 1815." *Maryland Historical Magazine,* 70, no. 4 (Winter 1975): 372–78.

Stump, William. "Joseph Sterett." *Sunday Sun* (Baltimore), October 21, 1949.

The Sun (Baltimore). "Baltimore's Proud Day, A Maryland Lady's Reminiscences." September 12, 1888.

———. "Caulk's Field Marker: Commemorative of a Battle in Kent County in 1812." October 19, 1902.

———. "City's Peril Recalled: Mute Reminders of Days of 1814…'Island Parson' Was a Hero." August 28, 1905.

———. "D.A.R. Gets Barney Relics." June 27, 1919.

———. "Died, Nathaniel Williams." May 10, 1859.

———. "Dr. Jacob Houck and the Battle of North Point." September 16, 1907.

———. "Find Two Skeletons: Building Erected in 1730 Was a Prison in Riots of 1812." March 9, 1905.

———. "Fishing for Cannon." May 2, 1873.

———. "Fort Nonsense." October 29, 1983.

———. "Fought at North Point: Nathaniel Williams Lived at Calvert and Lexington Streets." July 18, 1905.

———. "Historic Cannon Explodes." November 14, 1912.

———. "History Makers Great in Death." September 28, 1903.

———. "Injury of an Amateur Artilleryman." March 4, 1884.

———. "A 'Jug Wasps' Nest: Collector Riggin's Parlor Ornament—A Story of the War of 1812." January 11, 1898.

———. "Maryland Obituary, Mrs. Kinsey E. Thomas." February 2, 1900.

———. "Mrs. Louisa Sterett Hollins." October 7, 1889.

————. "Obituary." January 17, 1902.

————. "Offers Proof That Cock Did Crow at Ft. McHenry," September 15, 1932.

————. "Old Defenders Day." September 13, 1887.

————. "Painful Accident." July 11, 1843.

————. "The Parson of the Isles: An Eastern Sho' Worthy." October 21, 1906.

————. "Part of the Star-Spangled Banner Now Walker Heirloom." November 8, 1973.

————. "Peter Parker's Cannon: Kent County's Trophy Which She Captured from the British." 1899.

————. "A Precious Remnant." December 18, 1896.

————. "Recalls Queer Battle." July 12, 1909.

————. "Relic Buried with Her." January 18, 1902.

————. "A Relic Gone." March 22, 1844.

————. "A Relic of the War of 1812." April 17, 1884.

————. "Royal Oak's Historic Relics." May 12, 1885.

————. "The Soldiers Return." June 3, 1842.

————. "The Town of Royal Oak." April 14, 1907.

————. Knight's Obituary. August 10, 1913.

————. Nathaniel F. Williams Obituary. December 26, 1864.

————. Obituary. June 28, 1878.

————. Sister Mary Xavier Queen Obituary. December 6, 1906.

————. November 20, 1838.

————. October 12, 1880.

Svejda, George J. *History of the Star-Spangled Banner from 1814 to the Present.* National Park Service, 1969.

The Swampoodle Book: A Walk Back Through History—Lower Marlboro, Then and Now. Lower Marlboro, MD: Calvert County Public Schools, Calvert County Office on Aging, 1983.

Swann, Don, Jr., ed. *Colonial and Historical Houses of Maryland.* Baltimore: The Johns Hopkins University Press, 1975.

Taney, Roger Brooke. Introductory Letter Narrating the Incidents Connected with the Origin of the Song "The Star-Spangled Banner." In *Poems of the Late Francis S. Key.* New York: Robert Carter & Brothers, 1857.

Townsend, George Alfred. *Tales of the Chesapeake.* Cambridge, MD: Tidewater Publishers, 1968.

Trotten House vertical file. Dundalk Patapsco Neck Historical Society, Dundalk, Maryland.

Tucker, Lillian H. "Sir Peter Parker: Commander of HMS *Menelaus* in the Year 1814." *Bermuda Historical Quarterly* 1, no. 4 (October 1944): 189–95.

Unger, Harlow. *The Last Founding Father: James Monroe and a Nation's Call to Greatness.* New York: Da Capo Press, 2009.

United States Gazette (Philadelphia). July 2, 1814.

U.S. National Park Service. "Jean Lafitte: History and Mystery." Jean Lafitte National Historical Park and Preserve, http://www.nps.gov/jela/historyculture/upload/Jean-Lafitte-pirate-site-bulletin-for-the-web-Sep-2010.pdf.

Usilton, Fred G. "Battle of Caulk's Field." *Kent County News* (MD), August 26, 1964.

Virginia Argus. October 12, 1812.

———. September 17, 1812.

Virginia Patriot. December 8, 1812.

———. September 21, 1813.

Wallace, Reverend Adam. *The Parson of the Islands: A Biography of the Rev. Joshua Thomas.* Reprint of 1861 edition. Cambridge, MD: Tidewater Publishers, 1961.

Washington Herald. June 25, 1911.

Washington Post. "Bridge Burned by the British." March 9, 1902.

———. "What's This Classified Fort Nonsense." May 18, 1985.

Whitehouse Historical Association. *Saving History / Dolley Madison, the White House and the War of 1812.* http://www.whha.org/whha_classroom/classroom_documents-1812_a.html.

Whitelaw, Ralph T. *Virginia's Eastern Shore: A History of Northampton and Accomack Counties.* Gloucester, MA: Peter Smith, 1968.

Whitney, Weston, and Caroline Canfield Bullock. "Folklore from Maryland." *Memoirs of the American Folklore Society* 28 (1925).

Xavier, Sister Mary. *Grandma's Stories and Anecdotes of "Ye Olden Times": Incidents of the War of Independence, Etc.* Boston: Angel Guardian Press, 1899.

Youmans, Harold. "Eight Days in May: The British Raid on Fort Oswego, 1814." Lecture given May 8, 2010, at Fort Ontario State Historic Site, Owego, New York.

Young, James. *The Citizen Soldiers at North Point and Fort McHenry, September 12 & 13, 1814.* Baltimore: James Young, 1889.

ARCHIVAL MATERIAL

Library of Congress

Nicholson, Joseph H., to Secretary of War John Armstrong, September 18, 1814. Joseph Hopper Nicholson Papers.

Nicholson, Joseph H., to Monroe, September 1, 1814. James Monroe Papers.

Reed, Colonel Philip, to Major General Samuel Smith, September 18, 1814. Samuel Smith Papers.

"Remarks, &c., onboard HMS Albion, October 14, 1814." George Cockburn Papers, MSS 17576, reel 5, containers 7-8.

Simms, Charles to Nancy Simms, September 3, 1814. Charles Simms Papers, vol. 6. Peter Force Collection, Series 8D, fols. 35428-29 (reel 66).

Smith, Major General Samuel, to Major George Armistead, November 6, 1815. Samuel Smith Papers.

Maryland Historical Society (MdHS) Library

Hollingsworth, Lydia, to Ruth H., September 30, 1814. Hollingsworth Letters.

Nicholson, Joseph H., to Brigadier General William Winder, September 16. William Winder Papers.

Willis, General George R. "Sidelights on the Character of Gen. Robert Ross." Lecture given before MdHS, November 9, 1914.

Maryland Historical Trust

Historic Sites Inventory No.: AA-80. Location: David W. Taylor, NSRDC, Annapolis Laboratory, Church Road, Anne Arundel County.

Maryland State Archives (Annapolis)

"Bread and Cheese Creek." Provincial Court Land Records, 1770–1774.

Indenture of September 9, 1771. Provincial Court Land Records, 1770–1774.

"Proceedings of the Governor and Council." SC 3159, 585.

National Archives and Records Administration (Washington, D.C.)

Barney, Commodore Joshua, to Secretary of the Navy William Jones, August 29, 1814. NARA, RG45, Letters Received by the Secretary of Navy: Miscellaneous Letters, 1814, vol. 6, no. 57 (M124, roll no. 65).

National Archives United Kingdom (London)

Captain's Log, HMS Royal Oak. British Admiralty Records.

Crease, Lieutenant Henry, to Vice Admiral Sir Alexander F.I. Cochrane.

Logbook of HM frigate Surprise, September 7, 1814. British Admiralty Records.

"A Log of the proceedings of HM Ship Royal Oak, Joseph Pearce, Esq.," ADM 51/2760.

"Sketch of the Attack, [at Caulks Field], September 1,1814,"ADM 1/507.

National Library of Scotland (Edinburgh)

Claxton, Lieutenant Christopher, to Captain Thomas Hardy, September 16, 1814. Alexander Cochrane Papers.

"List of Officers, Seamen and Marines Killed, Wounded & Belonging to His Majesty's Ship Menelaus on the Morning of the 31 of August 1814. Henry Crease, Esq., Acting Commander, A.S. Missing, Surgeon." Alexander Cochrane Papers.

Parker, Captain Peter, to Vice Admiral Alexander Cochrane, August 29, 1814, Cochrane Papers.

Naval History and Historical Command (Washington Navy Yard)

Barrie, Robert, to Admiral John B. Warren, November 14, 1814, reprinted pp. 395–96.

Beckwith, Colonel Sir Thomas Sidney, to Admiral Sir John Borlace Warren, July 5, 1813, reprinted pp. 364–65.

Cockburn, Rear Admiral George, to Vice Admiral Alexander Cochrane, July 21, 1814, reprinted pp. 165.

Jones, William, Secretary of the Navy, to Congressman Richard M. Johnson, October 3, 1814, reprinted pp. 311–18.

The Naval War of 1812: A Documentary History, vol. 2, Ed. William S. Dudley (Washington: Naval Historical Center, 1992).

The Naval War of 1812: A Documentary History, Vol. 3 Ed. Michael J. Crawford (Washington: Naval Historical Center, 2002).

Tingey, Commodore Thomas, to Secretary of the Navy William Jones, November 9, 1814, reprinted pp. 320–21.

New-York Historical Society

Nicholson, Joseph H., to Mrs. Albert Gallatin, September 4, 1814. Gallatin Papers.

University of Pennsylvania (Philadelphia)

Nicholson, Joseph H., to Secretary of the Navy William Jones, August 28, 1814. William Jones Papers.

Index

About the Authors

Ralph Eshelman was co-director of the Patuxent River Cultural Resource Survey, which discovered and partially excavated a War of 1812 vessel from the U.S. Chesapeake Flotilla. He conducted a holistic inventory of War of 1812 sites in Maryland for the National Park Service's National Battlefield Protection Program and has published four books on the War of 1812. Eshelman was designated "Honorary Colonel of the Fort McHenry Guard" by the National Park Service in 2009. He currently serves as a consultant to the Star-Spangled Banner National Historic Trail. Eshelman has visited every known War of 1812 site in the Chesapeake Bay region and is considered among the leading experts on this resource base.

Scott S. Sheads has served as a ranger-historian and historic weapons officer at Fort McHenry National Monument and Historic Shrine in Baltimore since 1979. Scott served as a co-historian for the Smithsonian Institution's "Saving the Star-Spangled Banner Project" and for the National Park Service's "The Star-Spangled Banner National Historic Trail" feasibility study. He has published several books on the War of 1812 and the Civil War and has authored numerous journal articles for the *Maryland Historical Magazine*. Scott's most recent publication is *The Chesapeake Campaigns, 1813–1815: Middle Ground of the War of 1812* (Osprey Publications, Ltd., 2013).